BERLITZ

CRETE

- A ✓ in the text denotes a highly recommended sight
- A complete A–Z of practical information starts on p.107
- Extensive mapping throughout: on cover flaps and in text

Printed in Switzerland by Weber S.A., Bienne.

1st edition (1993/1994)

Although we make every effort to ensure the accuracy of the information in this guide, changes do occur. If you have any new information, suggestions or corrections to contribute, we would like to hear from you. Please write to Berlitz Publishing at the above address.

Text:	Jack Altman
Editor:	Sarah Hudson
Photography:	Jon Davison
Layout:	Visual Image
Cartography:	*Falk* Falk-Verlag, Hamburg
Thanks to:	The Greek National Tourist Organization for their valuable assistance in the preparation of this book.

CONTENTS

The Island and the People

It is not at all unusual to hear the proud people of Crete refer to their beloved island as a 'continent'. As a holiday destination, this richly varied island is as self-contained as its people are self-assured. Nowhere is it easier to combine lazing on a beach with cultural enrichment, or to indulge yourself with the best Greek seafood, cheese and wine, and then work them off with a bracing hike through the lovely meadows and mountains of the interior.

Crete is very much its own country. At a crossroads between the Middle East, Africa and the western Mediterranean, its civilization is the oldest in Europe. After centuries of courageous and often violent struggle against the Turks to achieve union with Greece, it now stands resolutely apart from it. Greece's largest island, it is Texas with a more ancient pride, a more cheerful Sicily, Scotland with more sun. Independent-minded people? Who else would name their sons *Eleftherios* – 'Freedom'?

In the Beginning

The Levantine and European roots of Cretan culture are 'documented' by Greek mythology. A princess of what is now Lebanon was walking down by the beach one day when she noticed among her father's prize herd of cattle a handsome, new, pure white bull. Playful rather than fierce, it let her ride on its back, feed it flowers, garland its horns. Suddenly it floated with her out to sea and swam to the island of Crete. There, the bull turned out to be Zeus in disguise, changed into an eagle and ravished the princess. The first son of the union was Minos, King of Knossós. The princess's name: Europa.

Europe's Bridge

The Cretans have good reason to be proud. On this island, you will be exploring the very cradle of civilization not just of Greece itself, but of all Europe. In the grandiose palace of Knossós – and the fine but more modest remains at Phaistós, Mália and Káto Zákros – you will walk among the vestiges of Minoan culture that blossomed from 3000 to 1400 BC. Excavated by Sir Arthur Evans at the turn of the century, Knossós set a tone in grace and dignity that would forever be the benchmark for the best in Western values. A grace and dignity imbued with a sensual charm and colour which Crete took from the

exotic kingdoms to the east and south.

The Sea of Crete rounds off the southern periphery of the Aegean, opening Europe to the influences of Asia and northern Africa. Crete's mountains prolong the south eastern sweep of the Peloponnese's Taigetos Range in the stepping stones that continue with Karpathos and Rhodes to the coast of Asia Minor. Do not be surprised to see subtropical flora – this land is closer to the equator than Tunis or Algiers.

Váï, on the north-east point of Crete, offers inviting seas and exciting landscapes.

7

*T*he beauty of the land is a constant pleasure on an island where for some, time hasn't changed a thing.

Africa is only 300 km (200 miles) across the Libyan Sea from Crete's south coast.

The long, narrow island – 250 km (155 miles) from west to east but only 60 km (37 miles) across at its widest point – is divided lengthways by a series of mountain ranges: to the west, the Levka or White Mountains, in the centre, the sacred peaks of Ida and Díkti – where Zeus spent his childhood – and the Sitía range at the eastern end of the island.

The Cretan people today are unquestionably the sum of their history. Their religion combines Greek Orthodox sobriety with pagan superstition. Poets like to imagine vestiges of ancient Minoan playfulness in the twinkle of an eye during a well-wined dinner. More in evidence is the sombre pride of survivors, born of centuries of resistance to Venetian, Turkish and – in living memory – German invaders. In the mountains, the diminishing communities of peasants show a certain stoicism in the face of the most recent invaders – tourists.

Bases for Exploration

The population of over half a million is concentrated mainly along the plains and gentler mountain slopes of the north

coast and is scattered only very sparsely on the south coast, where the mountains drop abruptly into the sea. As a result, most tourist facilities are clustered along the north coast, in and around Ágios Nikólaos, Eloúnda and Sitía to the east, outside Iráklion, the centrally located capital, and in and around Réthimnon, Chaniá and Kastélli to the west. They are all linked by the island's only major highway.

On the south coast, with Ierápetra the lone substantial town, you will find secluded spots at isolated fishing villages like Paleochóra and Chóra Sfakíon or, developing slowly but surely, the resorts of Mátala and Agía Galíni.

Unless you are just looking for a place in which to sit and soak up the sun or enjoy the watersports facilities, each town can be considered as a useful gateway from which to explore inland. Apart from its magnificent archaeological museum and old Venetian fortress, the principal asset of the bustling commercial town of Iráklion is its accessibility

to the neighbouring palace of Knossós. It is also the starting-point for trips south across the island to the Roman ruins of Górtis and Minoan sites of Phaistós and Agía Triáda.

The well-developed modern resorts of Ágios Nikólaos and its neighbours are ideal bases from which to visit the Toploú Monastery, the Minoan palaces of Mália and Káto

It's easy to lose yourself strolling around unspoilt Réthimnon and observing history put to use. **11**

FACTS AND FIGURES

Geography:
Crete *(Krìti)* is Greece's southernmost and largest island with an area of 8300 sq km (3200 sq miles). It is the fifth largest island in the Mediterranean after Sicily, Sardinia, Cyprus and Corsica. It lies some 260 km (160 miles) south of Athens and only 300 km (187 miles) north of Africa. Its most important river is the Geropotamos irrigating the farmland of the southern Messará Plain. Highest point: Mount Ida, 2456 m (8058 ft).

Population: 502,000

Major Towns:
Iráklion (115,000), Chaniá (50,000), Réthimnon (20,000), Ágios Nikólaos (8000)

Government:
Since the fall of the military dictatorship in 1974, Greece has been a presidential parliamentary republic of which Crete is one of ten administrative regions. The island comprises four prefectures *(nómoi)*: Iráklion, Chaniá, Réthimnon and Lasíthi. A local governor administers each prefecture, which sends to the Parliament in Athens deputies in numbers proportional to its population.

Religion:
Within the Christian Eastern Orthodox Church, claiming 98% of the population, the Cretan Church is administratively autonomous. It is headed by an Archbishop and seven metropolitans (senior to the patriarchs).

Zákros, the east coast beach of Váï and the mountain villages of the Díkti and Sitía ranges.

The old Venetian towns of Réthimnon and Chaniá are perfect for people with a taste for rambling, whether it be through the famous Samariá or Imbros gorges in the White Mountains or the lovely Amari valley winding around Mount Ida.

Away from the Madding Crowd

Nature-lovers will be in their element here. For amateur botanists, Crete boasts some 130 species of plant life unique to the island. Ask at the main tourist offices about guided tours. In early spring, you will see orchids and listera, fields of crocus and anemone, and later narcissus, wild tulips, and vast carpets of buttercups in the upland meadows of the Ida and White Mountains.

While the city markets are full of oranges (the subject of connoisseur's odes), you'll also find figs, apricots, almonds, pomegranates, and every kind of olive. All these grow wild in the hills and valleys as well.

Bird-watchers come for the spring migration: egrets, golden orioles, falcons and kingfishers. Birds for whom Crete is home include eagles, buzzards, bearded vultures, blue rock thrushes, and owls. You may spot ibex goats in the mountains, weasels and the odd badger. Nastier, but not frequent, are scorpions and vipers.

A Few Home Truths

When the apostle Paul made his disciple Titus first bishop of Crete, he wrote him a letter warning him the job would be tough. These Cretans spelled trouble, 'Unruly and vain talkers and deceivers,' said Paul, 'whose mouths must be stopped, who subvert whole houses, teaching things which they ought not. One of themselves, even a prophet of their own, said: "The Cretans are always liars, evil beasts.".'This witness is true.'

A Brief History

Unlike more recent Turkish invaders, settlers from Anatolia (the southern region of modern day Turkey) had a beneficial influence on the island's earliest inhabitants. Successive waves of cultivators brought bronze artefacts and the plough, adding a richer diet of olives, figs and vines to the meagre cereal crops of their predecessors.

With its well-farmed soil and cattle pastures, the great island enjoyed peace and prosperity in the early days, untroubled by the invasions that swept through mainland Greece. The rise to the era of Minoan civilization began around 3000 BC. Cretans carried on a brisk trade

A Fair Amount of Bull

Many a Greek myth has behind it a hard political fact. Historians believe the legend of Athens' obligation to sacrifice seven young men and seven maidens to the Minotaur refers to a time when Crete reigned supreme in the Aegean and Athens had to pay heavy tribute.

The Minotaur was the offspring of a torrid affair that King Minos's wife Pasiphak had with a bull. Understandably upset, Minos had the bull-headed monster hidden with a human body in a labyrinth. At nine-year intervals, to keep the creature happy – after all, the Minotaur was family – the powerful monarch fed him 14 young men and girls from Athens.

One of the victims, Theseus, Athenian hero and son of the King of Athens, put a stop to it. He seduced the king's daughter Ariadne, who gave him a ball of wool with which to find his way out of the labyrinth after killing her monstrous half-brother. On his way back to Athens, however, without so much as a second thought, Theseus left Ariadne, pregnant, stranded on Náxos. Heroes are not always gentlemen.

with the Middle East and Egypt, as well as the other Greek islands, with an emphasis on luxury goods: ivory, delicate pottery and fine gold jewellery.

Golden Age of Minos

Fearing no enemies, the Cretans built their first palaces without fortifications at Knossós, Phaistós and Mália around 2000 BC. It is not clear whether war or earthquake caused the palaces' first destruction 300 years later, but they were rebuilt even bigger and more splendid. Designs were still

King Minos' decorative palace at Knossós. The Minoans made even storage jars ornate. **15**

strictly for pleasure: decorative entrances, roof terraces facing the beautiful surrounding countryside, ornately frescoed bedrooms, sophisticated plumbing for the bathrooms and barbecue braziers in the kitchens.

Crete's Minoan civilization, named after the mythical King Minos of Knossós, was generally on a very human scale. In small sanctuaries or intimate palace chapels, Cretans worshipped female deities which were sculpted in small figurines rather than great statues. The goddesses' symbol was the famous double axe. Male deities served as subordinate consorts, with the bull as their emblem.

In the palaces' sculptures and paintings, the overall tone is of warm sensuality, drawing inspiration from the island's Egyptian and other Middle Eastern neighbours. But Minoan art is also infused with the Cretans' own distinctively lively sense of colour, movement and humour.

At their height, the people of Minoan Crete probably numbered over two million, about four times more than today's population, with 100,000 in Knossós alone.

They were one of the Mediterranean's great naval powers, with wood from the vast cypress forests, which then covered the island, providing the raw material for their boats. But they concentrated their power far more on the commercial than the military, serving the islanders' taste for the good life, rather than any hunger for a new empire.

The rich land produced enough wine, olive oil and honey for export. Copper and tin were imported for bronze and refashioned by skilled Minoan artists for export. In order to make their decorative, elegant jewellery, they bought lapis lazuli from Afghanistan, ivory from Syria, and gold, silver and black obsidian from Anatolia.

Recently discovered artefacts now suggest that Minoan sailors could even have passed through the Straits of Gibraltar and reached as far north as Scandinavia.

Dorians and Romans

In 1500 BC, Dorian invaders from the Balkans drove south through the Greek mainland and across to Crete. The tall, blond northerners over-ran the island and the brilliant Minoan civilization went into decline. A century later the palace of Knossós was des-troyed by an earthquake and Crete withdrew from the centre stage of Greek history.

While some coastal dwell-ers migrated to remote moun-tain refuges, others embarked on an overseas exodus that took them as far as Palestine, where – ultimate humiliation – the Israelites referred to them as Philistines. The island did

Bull-leaping was considered an honourable skill. This fresco shows an acrobat in full leap, preparing for the final victorious somersault.

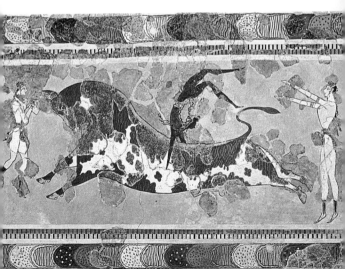

*C*opies of the Phaistós Disk, unearthed at Phaistós Palace, are sold each year. The Sainte Vierge (right) is just one of the many beautiful icons at the 14th-century Toploú Monastery.

not get involved in Greece's Persian and Peloponnesian Wars, but attracted Alexander's attention as a valuable source of brave and energetic mercenaries.

Crete remained a province of the Roman Empire from 67 BC to AD 395, with Górtis as its capital. The only major feature surviving from the period preceding the Roman occupation is the incredible Code of Laws inscribed on a monumental stone tablet at Górtis (see p.45).

With them, the Romans managed to bring a certain order to the island, putting an end to internal struggles, building new roads and aqueducts and introducing systems of domestic plumbing and central heating not greatly inferior to those found today.

Christian Birthpains

In the early days following the advent to the island of the apostle Paul with his disciple Titus in AD 59, Christianity had a hard time combatting the Cretans' pagan beliefs. It finally triumphed (although still not completely immune from its ancient superstitions) to achieve the fierce Orthodoxy of today.

When Roman power split into two, the Byzantine Empire inherited the island and slowly won the Cretans' loyal support. They remained faithful to the Orthodox Church throughout the Arabs occupation of the island from AD 824 to 961.

The Arabs systematically destroyed the churches and turned the island into a pirate base and one of the Mediterranean's major slave markets. Their fortified capital at Rabd-el-Kandek (later called Candia to western Europe, and now known as Iráklion).

When recapturing the island, the Byzantine commander, Nikephóros Phokás, was no more tenderhearted. In an attempt to impress the Arabs holding out in the fort, he catapulted his Moslem prisoners' heads over the wall. The lucky ones became slaves.

Venetian Days

After Byzantium fell to the Crusaders, Crete was given to Boniface of Montferrat who sold it for cash – the sum of 1000 silver marks – to Venice. Crete thrived under the 465 years of Venetian occupation (1204-1669). As a valuable source of ship-building timber in a key strategic location, the island was a kingpin in the farflung commercial empire and became the Republic's first formally constituted overseas colony. Proudly embla- **19**

zoned with the Lion of St Mark, the ports and fortifications of Chaniá, Réthimnon and Iráklion bear witness to the Venetians' ambitious and decorative public building programme. Several handsome villas also attest to their gracious style of living.

Typically, the Cretans at first resisted the new foreign rulers with bloody revolts, but then settled down to intermarry with the occupiers and even participate in their style of government. They were certainly better off than the Armenian and Georgian slaves brought in from the Caucasus to work the Venetians' vast sugar plantations.

The arts flourished in the 16th and 17th centuries. The great literary figure of the time, Vitsénzos Kornáros, wrote a long romantic epic poem in the Cretan dialect, *Erotòkritos.* Even if it has since lost its traditional hold in the mountain villages, it is still declaimed among the *literati* of Réthimnon.

Crete was a refuge for Greek artists fleeing from the

*S*ailing has long been a part of life on Crete. Chaniá's light-house makes a perfect backdrop.

Turkish conquest of Constantinople in 1453, but two of the great painters of the 16th century were both Cretan, born in Iráklion. One of the most accomplished creators of Greek icons, Michaïl Damaskinós, combined Byzantine convention with a more audacious technique he had studied in Venice.

His more illustrious contemporary was Domínikos Theotokópoulos, the son of a tax-collector who had converted to Catholicism. He began with icons and went off to Italy, then Spain, where he made his name, slightly more famously, as El Greco.

The Battle for Crete

The Turks waged a titanic struggle to wrest Crete from the Venetians. It began with raids on Chaniá and Sitía in the 1530s by the notorious pirate Barbarossa Khair ed-Din, sailing from Algeria.

Over the next century, the Venetians strengthened the fortifications of what they saw as the last Christian bastion against Turkey's advance in the western Mediterranean. But Chaniá and Réthimnon fell in 1645.

Two years later, the Turks laid siege to the capital, Candia (Iráklion), whose small civilian population of 12,000 was already beset by the plague. The siege was to last 22 years. After the first 15 years, the Turkish commander, Hussein Pasha, was summoned back to Constantinople and publicly strangled for his failure to take the city.

In spite of their Christian allies' perennial reluctance to send adequate support (most notably the bombastic effort of Louis XIV's troops led by the Duc de Beaufort a year before the end), the Venetians' resistance was prodigious. The city's capture in 1669 resulted in the deaths of 30,000 Venetians and 118,000 Turks. As the conquerors entered by the city gates, the Venetians made a negotiated orderly departure, taking with them the cherished head of Saint Titus. This relic of the island's patron saint was only returned in 1966.

21

Turkish Rule

Crete's years spent under the Turks (1669-1898) were a period of cultural and economic stagnation. After the occasionally oppressive, but often brilliant, centuries of Venetian government, Crete slid back into the dark ages. The rule of the pashas was both exacting and indolent, allowing culture, the buildings, roads and the island itself to deteriorate. They built no new mosques, preferring to convert existing churches and leaving only a few houses and ornate street fountains as vestiges of their presence. Their cuisine and coffee could be considered their most lasting and appreciated legacy.

The darkness was broken only by outbursts of revolt launched from mountain strongholds – for which communities in the plains paid a high price in the form of bloody reprisals. Once Greece had achieved independence from the Ottoman Empire after the war of 1821, Crete had to endure nearly a century more of humiliating subjection to Turkish oppression and the whims of the Great Powers.

The ferocity of the Cretan combat against the Turks, proclaiming 'freedom or death', had all the trademarks of their fiercely independent (some may say almost masochistic) spirit. Violent insurrection provoked equally violent massacres in retaliation. The savage deaths became a collective badge of honour of epic proportions, not unlike the legendary glory attributed to ancient Greek exploits in the Trojan Wars.

The island's perennial suffering was duly celebrated in the popular heroic *Songs of Dighenis* (adapted from their medieval origins for the modern struggle), Pandelis Prevelakis' grim novel, *The Cretan*, and the lofty novels and memoirs of Níkos Kazantzákis (see also p.30).

Agios Nikólaos, once a quiet harbour town, has developed with style and grace.

Union with Greece

The European powers forced the Turks to grant the island autonomy within the Ottoman Empire and accept Prince George, second son of the Greek king, as governor. But it was only in 1913, under the leadership of Greece's great statesman, Elefthérios Venizélos, a native son of Crete, that *ènosis* (union) was finally achieved.

Crete was reunited with Greece as part of the Bucharest settlement ending the Balkan Wars. The 10,000 remaining Turks were finally evacuated in 1923 after the Treaty of Lausanne. Under a clause exchanging populations, 13,000 Greek (and Armenian) refugees from Turkey chose to settle in Crete.

Agricultural resources were improved and Sir Arthur Evans' discoveries at Knossós (see also p.36) and subsequent dramatic excavations of other Minoan palaces brought a new prosperity with the increase of the 20th-century phenomenon of tourism.

But Crete's pains were not at an end. During World War II, the rapid advance of the German forces through Greece in 1941 forced the Allies to retreat to Crete. Then, in a 10-day battle, British, Australian and New Zealand soldiers joined Cretan militia in a valiant, but ultimately vain, attempt to defend the island. Allied losses numbered 2000 killed and 12,000 taken prisoner before evacuating their remaining troops. With a centuries-old tradition of resistance to foreign invaders, Cretans maintained constant guerrilla warfare which made the German occupation expensive and uncomfortable.

After the war, much of the island was left in ruins from heavy bombing, and in places succumbed to the hasty post-war building boom. However, today, with luck, its most caring citizens have discovered the importance of preserving the island's magnificent natural beauty, the culture of its grandiose past, and the taste of their Minoan ancestors for the gracious good life.

Where to Go

Deciding on where to go in Crete usually depends on the importance you attach to the three basic reasons for heading there in the first place: soaking up the sun and sea, visiting the ancient and Byzantine monuments, or getting to know the people and the island itself. Some visitors plump for one at the expense of the other two. To enjoy Crete to the full, we recommend a combination of all three.

However forbidding (or dull) you may imagine ancient ruins to be, the great monumental sites like the Palace of Knossós exert a mysterious power on even the most blasé imagination. Quite apart from the mystic attractions of the Byzantine churches and their icons, the moment of meditation there is cooling for both body and spirit alike. Taken in small doses before the heat of the day sets in, these ancient and medieval monuments can act as a tonic if sunbathing threatens to addle your brain.

We have divided the island up into four sections: Iráklion; Knossós and the other major archaeological sites of Central Crete; the coastal resorts and mountain villages of Eastern Crete (around Ágios Nikólaos); and Western Crete's resorts (Réthimnon, Chaniá) and mountain excursions.

WHICH SEASON?

Crete has a somewhat short spring, sweltering summer, and cooler autumn, but even winter temperatures rarely drop below 8°C (46°F). Mass

Unfinished Business

People wonder about the rusting steel rods sticking out of roofs which give the island's modern buildings an unkempt, unfinished look. It is quite intentional. Finishing off a house with a proper roof would cost the owner extra property taxes.

tourist traffic in the high season makes May, June and September the most attractive months for easy movement around the island. Spring is also the best time to enjoy its mountain greenery and wild flowers. Whenever the coastal heat gets too great, plan an excursion to the cooler mountain villages.

From time to time, the sultry stillness of summer is buffeted between mid-July and the end of August by the Aegean's notorious *méltemi* wind. This north-west wind starts around 8 a.m. and peters out at sunset.

Remember that wherever you find yourself in summer, one institution remains sacred – the siesta. Apart from a few crazy businessmen in Iráklion, all Cretans will rest between 3 and 5 p.m. Don't try to beat them – join them!

GOING NATIVE

Greeks are delighted to discover any foreigner speaking their language. They usually manage a little English, German, French or Italian, roughly in that order, but will immediately be well disposed to you if you try at least a couple of Greek words to show willing. We propose some useful phrases on the cover of this guide (and for more ambitious use there is also the Berlitz *Greek for Travellers* phrase book and dictionary).

Iráklion

With its busy airport only 4 km (2¹/₂ miles) from the city, the island capital is a lively, but also noisy, centre of commerce and industry. Its population of 115,000 places it fifth among Greek cities, and first in terms of income per capita. If it does not invite a prolonged stay, it certainly has plenty to offer for a visit of a day or two, with the Venetian legacy of harbour, castle and ramparts, the church of Agía Ekateríni with its great icons by Michaïl Damaskinós,

A popular excursion from Ágios Nikólaos is to secluded, atmospheric Spinalonga Island.

and, above all, a collection of Minoan treasures which make the Archaeological Museum a proud rival to Athens' National Museum. Iráklion also has the best selection of jewellery, ceramics and other souvenirs.

The best way to enjoy these attractions is to make excursions *into* the town from a coastal resort. Reserve one day for the Archaeological Museum and other cultural sights and perhaps a second day to go shopping or to visit the market to make up a picnic for the mountains.

The few fellows you may see in traditional costume – black scarf, blouse and cummerbund over *vráka* breeches tucked into knee-high boots – are the real thing, not a tourist office gimmick.

The Town

The city centre's charm has not been enhanced by centuries of earthquakes (the last major one in 1926), World War II bombardment, and least of all by unimaginative building in reinforced concrete. But some of the surviving spirit of the town – *megalo kastro* (great fortress) to its older residents – can be captured on a stroll around the port. The new outer harbour bustles with ferries and freighters. The inner Venetian harbour is now reserved for a busy traffic of fishing boats, yachts and caïques.

Towering over them out on the jetty is the grand **Venetian Fort** (*Rocca al Mare* to the Italians, *Koúles* to the Turks). Built between 1523 and 1549, its massive buff-stone walls provided the main bulwark of the Venetians' heroic resistance to the Turks' prolonged 17th-century assault. Climb up to the battlements for a fine view over the harbour and the Sea of Crete. Emblazoned on a fortress wall facing the sea is the best preserved of three sculptured lions of St Mark, proud emblem of the former Adriatic city-state.

On the quay across the street from the harbour auth-

The Name Game

There is no hard and fast rule for the Roman-lettered versions of Greek names on signposts and road maps. You should have no problem with Heraklion and Iráklion, but what we call Chaniá may also turn up as Haniá, Khaniá and even Xaniá.

We have used the names most generally accepted in western Europe, but be prepared for variations. Finding your way around towns off the tourists' beaten track will be much easier if you familiarize yourself with the Greek alphabet (see p.110) All street signs are written in capital letters. The words for street (*odós*), avenue (*leofóros*), and square (*platía*) are used in conversation but usually omitted from maps and signs.

ority are the lofty arcades and store-rooms of the 16th-century **arsenali** where ships were repaired and fitted out in preparation for battle on the high seas. From behind the harbour bus station, you can walk around the **Venetian walls** encircling the city. The promenade is about 4 km (2½ miles) long and affords dramatic and panoramic views of Iráklion. The ramparts run south past a pleasant public park to the **Promachón Mart-inéngo** (Martinengo Bastion), burial place of Crete's great 20th-century novelist Níkos Kazantzákis (see p.30).

The busy **Platía Venizélou** (Venizelos Square) is a good place to buy your souvenirs or read a newspaper at one of the many cafés – where you should also sample the local *bougátsa* (custard-filled pastry). Celebrating the Cretan-born Greek Prime Minister, Elefthérios Venizélos, who successfully fought for the island's union

*T*he port of Iráklion and its imposing Venetian fortress attracts ships from all over the Mediterranean and beyond.

(*ènosis*) with Greece, the square has long been the focus of the town's perennially heated political discussions, as well as more subtle traditional family negotiations for unions of a marital nature. In the centre, four lions support the ornate **Morosini Fountain** (1628), named after a former Venetian governor.

Across from the fountain stands the **Basilica of Ágios Márkos** (St Mark). Originally built under the Venetians in 1239, it suffered the vicissitudes of earthquakes and conversion to a mosque by the Turks before recovering its Venetian character in a restoration of the 1960s.

The interior offers a series of reproductions of magnificent 13th-, 14th- and 15th-century frescoes taken from the island's churches. The display makes a good introduction to the Cretan style of religious art.

At the beginning of Odós 25 Avgoústou (August 25th Street), the handsome arcaded 17th-century Venetian **loggia** has been reconstructed, adjoining the old armoury which now serves as the **Dimarkheíon**

Níkos Kazantzákis (1885-1957)

In Crete, said his father, writing books was work fit only for eunuchs and monks. Old Kazantzákis had been a fierce fighter in the last years of the struggle for the island's freedom from the Turks, and before him, the writer's grandfather had been a roistering brigand. Compensating for his lack of violent physical prowess, the author of *Zorba the Greek* and *The Last Temptation of Christ* filled his books with a lust for life and paroxysms of spiritual torment.

Born in Iráklion, Kazantzákis's life was a constant struggle to conquer the demands of his flesh and ease the suffering of his soul, happy in the end to be able to compose the poignant epitaph for his grave: 'I hope for nothing. I fear nothing. I am free.'

(City Hall). Behind them, the **Church of Ágios Títos**, also converted back from a Turkish mosque, provides a resumé of the island's history through its differing architectural styles, each added by the occupying power of the day. It is dedicated to the island's patron saint, Titus, a disciple of the apostle Paul. His skull, which the church keeps in a reliquary, was carried off to Venice for safe-keeping when the Turks captured Iráklion in 1669 and wasn't returned until 1966.

Down on the other side of Odós 25 Avgoústou, opposite the loggia, everyone (and especially parents) will be grateful for the children's playground in the **Párko El Gréko**.

From Platía Venizélou, moving away from the harbour, take the main shopping thoroughfare of Leofóros Kalokerinoú towards the three churches on Platías Agías Ekaterínis. On the west side of the square, the 19th-century cathedral and the more charming little church next to it are both dedicated to Ágios Minás. But the main attraction is the 16th-century **church of Agía Ekateríni** (St Catherine). Linked to the St Catherine's desert monastery at Mount Sinai, the church and its seminary provided a haven for artists and theologians fleeing the Turks in Constantinople.

The church is now a museum including six **icons** by Michaïl Damaskinós, true masterpieces of the art. Profiting from five years in Venice (1577-1582), the painter infused traditional Byzantine art with the Venetian school's renowned energy and bold use of colour. In the central nave you will find his *Adoration of the Magi, The Last Supper, The Virgin with Moses' Burning Bush, Christ with the Holy Women, Constantine with the Bishops,* and *Christ Celebrating Mass with the Angels.*

The **central market** is located on and around Odós 1866 (Cretans like to name their streets after dates marking important steps on their march to freedom – 1866 was the year the Arkádi Monastery was blown up – see p.74). Stalls of fruit and vegetables, exotic spices and the island's **31**

The early 18th-century church of Ágios Minás is dedicated to Iráklion's patron saint.

handily but noisily near the airport. Unless you are thinking of one last dip in the sea before your flight, be patient and head for a resort.

Archaeological Museum

People often prefer to tour an archaeological site before visiting the museum displaying its excavated artworks. In the case of Knossós, Phaistós, Agía Triáda and Crete's other Minoan archaeological sites, you will more easily appreciate their significance if you first visit Iráklion's magnificent **Archeologikó Mousío** (Archaeological Museum).

The elegance and vitality of life in the days of King Minos will seem more real after you have seen the beautifully exhibited Minoan treasures, along with scale-models

delicious honey and fresh yoghurt are succeeded by meat and fish markets of astonishing variety. At the top of the market street, on Platía Kornárou, take a rest at the café whose centrepiece is a kiosk formed from an old Turkish fountain. Behind is the 16th-century **Bembo Fountain** with its headless Roman statue found at Ierápetra.

If the fountain makes you long for a swim, the closest place is the popular **Karterós** (Florida Beach) at Amnissos,

of how the palaces probably looked in their heyday. For a complete sense of the sites, many visitors like to make a quick preliminary tour of the museum first and then a second, more leisurely tour after visiting the sites themselves.

More preoccupied with resisting earthquakes than appealing to the eye, the museum is an uninspiring concrete blockhouse. But its collection of Minoan art is the most complete in the world. Here are the highlights from its 20 galleries:

Gallery 2: from the first palaces (1900-1700 BC), look for the **town mosaics**, small earthenware plaques from Knossós bearing models of flat-roofed Minoan houses of up to three storeys, many with a rooftop attic. These will give you a good idea of what the houses excavated from the town of Gourniá looked like (see also p.55).

*L*e Prince, in Iráklion's Archaeological Museum, is testament to the Minoan's grace and charm.

Gallery 3: also from the early palace period, the famous **Phaistós Disk** from Phaistós Palace. The clay disk, 16 cm (6 in) in diameter, is covered on both sides with a so-far undeciphered hieroglyphic inscription spiralling to the centre. Its 241 miniature figures include vases, animals, birds, fish, insects and ships as well as men, women and children. What may be a religious hymn or magical incantation is now

reproduced all over the island as earrings, key chains, even cocktail coasters.

Gallery 4: from Knossós's golden Neopalatial age (1700-1450 BC), are two polychrome faïence figures of **snake goddesses** or priestesses, perhaps mother and daughter. In carefree Minoan fashion, they are bare-breasted. Snakes coil around one's tiara and waist, while the other has a small leopard on her cap and brandishes a snake in each hand. The ivory statue of a **bull-leaping acrobat** shows him in full flight in an audacious athletic ritual involving the bull, a central figure of Minoan culture. The bull, symbol of virility, is represented here in the striking black steatite, the **Bull's Head Chalice**, used for sacred libations poured through the mouth and the crown of the head.

Gallery 7: also Neopalatial, stone vases from Agía Triáda are remarkable for their vivid carving. The **Chieftain Cup** shows a chief receiving a gift of animal hides from a hunt or sacrifice. Liveliest of all is the **Harvester Vase**, shaped like an ostrich egg, with a rustic scene of peasants laughing and singing behind a priest, and musicians in a ritual autumn harvest procession.

Gallery 14: in this **Hall of Frescoes**, among the most significant is the series which decorates the 3000 year-old **Sarcophagus of Agía Triáda**, cut from a single limestone block. One side shows, to the right, a funeral procession in which a personification of the deceased receives offerings, probably for his voyage to the Land of the Dead; and to the left, women peforming a purification rite between two pillars topped by the sacred Minoan double-headed axe.

From the famous frescoes found at Knossós, an almond-eyed priestess or goddess was nicknamed *La Parisienne* by her discoverer, Sir Arthur Evans. Her elaborate coiffure and sensual red mouth recalls

Carefree Minoan women captured on a fresco found in excavations at Knossós.

the coquettes of the Belle Epoque. More demure are the pretty *Ladies in Blue*. The delicate *Prince of the Lilies* does not look as if he would fare very well in the bull-leaping (see also p.42) depicted in the *Toreador Fresco*.

Historical Museum

On the other side of town, across from the Xenía Hotel, the **Istorikó Mousío** (Historical Museum) takes up the story of Crete after the fall of the Minoans. The collections include Early Christian sculpture from Górtis, Byzantine icons, bronze liturgical instruments and frescoes. Explore the cosmopolitan character of Cretan society through Venetian sculptures from Iráklion's 17th-century loggia, the Hebrew coat of arms of a Venetian Jewish family, and 18th-century Turkish tombstones and frescoes.

Pride of place on the ground floor goes to an early picture by the city's most famous son,

El Greco. In 1569, when he was still just Domínikos Theotokópoulos, he painted this imaginary version of the St Catherine Monastery at the foot of Mount Sinai, one of the holiest shrines of the Orthodox church (and linked to the church of Ágia Ekateríni in Iráklion).

The island's battles are amply illustrated by collections of Venetian and French weapons and armour from the siege of Iráklion, the guns of Crete's War of Independence against the Turks, German helmets, parachutes and Nazi flags from World War II.

Upstairs are reconstructions of the studies of two local heroes – Emmanuel Tsouderis, Réthimnon-born Prime Minister during World War II, and Níkos Kazantzákis, with the author's desk, manuscripts, his library, photographs and other personal memorabilia. On the top floor, traditional Cretan communities are represented by typical peasant dwellings with utensils, costumes and fabrics taken from mountain villages on Ida and Díkti.

Central Crete

In the valleys between the Ida and Lasíthi mountains, the Minoan nobility built their earliest road linking their summer residences at Knossós and winter homes at Phaistós and Agía Triáda.

Roughly the same route is followed today to the island's principal archaeological sites of Knossós, Górtis, Phaistós and Agía Triáda – and beyond to the beautiful seaside resorts on the south coast.

Knossós needs a day to itself. The others can be comfortably combined in one excursion (tourist agencies run guided tours), with the bonus of a swim at Mátala or Agía Galíni.

KNOSSOS

Just 5 km (3 miles) south of Iráklion, you enter the excavated palace of King Minos under an arcade of magenta bougainvillea. There in the **west court** is a bronze bust of Sir Arthur Evans, the man who first uncovered and reconstructed the Minoan world of Knossós. Notice how the stone blocks of the palace's western façade were blackened by the fire of its destruction, probably by earthquake around 1500 BC.

Within minutes, tourists penetrating the palace precincts arrive at the conclusion that students of antiquity took years to reach – the palace of Knossós is itself laid out like the kind of labyrinth in which King Minos imprisoned the Minotaur (see p.14). Narrow zigzagging passages, broad corridors, stairways with L-shaped, T-shaped and X-shaped landings lead up and down and in and out of courtyards and vestibules among the palace's approximately 1200 rooms.

Just when you think you have got to the heart of the palace, the great central court, the corridor deviates away from it. You will find that a stairway leading out will simply double back, at which point you'll swear you hear the ghost of Minos snicker. Various theories suggest that the intricate layout was a deliberate plan to foil invading enemies or evil spirits. Some gloomy scholars have suggested that Knossós was not a palace at all, but a giant mausoleum like the Egyptian pyramids, in which following the complicated layout was part of a sacred ritual. Or is the maze simply a natural creation of the Minoans' sense of play which is so wonderfully depicted in their art?

Adopting the latter theory as the most attractive, the game, then, is to get to the central court. It can be done. Leaving Sir Arthur behind you, turn right (south) and take the **corridor of processions**. The frescoes here, like others on the site, are 'recreations' by the Gilliérons, a Swiss father and son team, of originals preserved in Iráklion's Archaeological Museum. They serve to clarify the functions and settings of what would otherwise be very anonymous, unadorned stones. Here, like others before them, two curly-haired, dark-skinned Minoans in loin cloths are shown carrying vessels towards the centre of the palace.

37

Turn left (east) towards the columned vestibule of the **south propylaea**. Note the characteristic downward taper of the reconstructed columns. A grand staircase leads north up to what Evans called the **piano nobile**, borrowing a term from the Italian Renaissance period for the loftier reception rooms of an upper storey. A balcony here gives you your first view of the central court.

Continue north via the palace's **sanctuary**. In keeping with the intimate, human

The Diggers

Director of Oxford's Ashmolean Museum, Sir Arthur Evans (1851-1941), began scratching around Knossós in 1894. Hoping to solve the linguistic riddles of Greece's earliest settlements, he was looking for clay tablets with pictographic inscriptions and engraved seal stones like those found on Mycenaean sites in the Peloponnese.

Some 16 years earlier, a local amateur archaeologist with the appropriate name of Mínos Kalokairinós had unearthed what Evans later identified as the Minoan palace's storerooms. The Turkish authorities stopped the excavations, but the discovery attracted the attention of the eccentric German digger Heinrich Schliemann, the obsessive excavator of Troy and Mycenae. Like some latterday Agamemnon avid to hold on to the spoils of past battles, Schliemann haggled over the price of the land, even the number of olive trees, and abandoned the site in high dudgeon in 1886.

Evans arrived with money, energy, vision and a little more diplomatic skill than Schliemann. After Crete won its autonomy, he was given a free hand to dig at leisure. From 1900 to 1940 he toiled away on the hillside he bought in the Kaíratos Valley, intent on discovering the fabled clay tablets and seal stones. He turned up relatively few, but managed to content himself with the colossal task of excavating and reconstructing the stupendous treasure trove of King Minos's palace.

scale of their lives, the Minoans did not have monumental temples for their worship but preferred the small shrines and chapels you will see here.

Immediately left (north) of a stairway leading into the central court is the entrance, via an antechamber with a marble basin, to the **throne room**. In front is a sunken area for purification rites. On the other side of the sanctuary's staircase is a columned **crypt and treasury** where various cult objects were excavated, including the snake-goddesses now in Iráklion's Archaeological Museum. It is believed that the sacred snakes had their home here.

Time now to stroll around the grand **central court**, 53 m (174 ft) long and 26 m (87 ft) wide, and imagine the scenes witnessed here 4000 years ago. This is where they held the athletic contests and great bull-leaping rituals so vividly depicted in the frescoes and sculptures.

Picture the buildings surrounding the court topped by symbolic bull-horns. Tiers of

*S*ir Arthur Evans spent a large part of his own fortune on dedicated excavations at Knossós.

spectators gather in open-air galleries supported on blood-red, gold-banded columns. Festive throngs of Minoan women spectators fan themselves with white ostrich plumes, their doe-eyes outlined and shadowed with green malachite, their reddened lips high- **39**

1 West Entrance
2 Corridor of the Procession
3 South Propylaeum
4 Stairway to Piano Nobile
5 Stairway to Central Court
6 Central Court
7 Throne Room
8 Storerooms
9 Shrine Rooms
10 Grand Staircase
11 Hall of Double Axes
12 Queen's Hall
13 Queen's Bathroom
14 Queen's Toilet
15 Prince of the Lilies Corridor
16 South House
17 Altar
18 Theatre
19 Lustral Area
20 North Portico, Bull Fresco
21 Pithi Storeroom

lighted against white face paint. Nestling in their elaborate, curled hair, jewels and pendants sparkle in the sunlight. The Minoan men are relaxed and casual, their equally elaborate and bejewelled coiffures framing eyes also accentuated by make-up. Deeply tanned, their lithe, muscular bodies are covered only by loincloths with tasselled codpieces. Music emanating from flutes and lyres spills across the courtyard to accompany the lively dancers and cart-wheeling acrobats. Leather-helmeted boxers fight in the blazing sun. Fans toss cascades of flowers into the ring for the victor.

Partly reconstructed, the palace of King Minos evokes the splendour of that ancient court. **41**

A hush falls over the spectators. Across the courtyard, the doors of the sanctuary open and a wide-eyed priestess emerges with writhing snakes in each hand. She intones an incantation, a blessing for the day's main event: the bull-leaping. The priestess withdraws and athletes enter the arena with the first bull. The nervous creature is steadied by two female athletes standing at the head and tail.

Hoisting himself up by grasping the bull by the horns, the first acrobat leaps headlong over the beast's back and then propels himself off the beast's haunches for a final somersault onto the ground. The crowd roars its appreciation as one acrobat after another lands on his feet. Then, suddenly, there is a chorus of gasps as the bull balks and tosses his head and the acrobat is impaled on his horns – a terrible, but honourable death. Later, the bulls themselves are sacrificed and roasted, by torchlight, for the evening feast, honouring both survivors and the dead.

On the east side of the court, opposite the sanctuary, a staircase leads down to what Evans identified as the **royal chambers**. These are the best-preserved rooms. Set into the slope of the hill, the quarters were built on four floors, two above and two below the level of the central court. Lighting was channelled down to rooms on lower floors through an ingenious system of spacious light wells.

Shields in a figure of eight shape, and signs of the Minoan double axe, mark the walls of what was probably the guard-room adjacent to the **king's chamber**, where Evans found a wooden throne. A narrow passage leads across to the **queen's chamber**, decorated by a fresco of dolphins and flying fish. Next to it is a room housing a clay bathtub and a toilet, originally equipped with a wooden seat and a still visible flushing system much admired by modern plumbers.

Head north of the royal quarters to the **storehouses and workshops** used by the palace's tailors, goldsmiths,

The gentle fresco of dolphins suggests that Sir Arthur Evans was correct in assigning this as the queen's chamber (or megaron).

potters and stone-masons. In particular, notice the enormous earthenware jars (*píthoi*), used for storing grain, oil and wine and big enough for a man to hide in – or drown in, as Minos's son Glaucus discovered to his cost when trying to help himself to honey.

Leave the main palace through the **north entrance**. North west of the palace is a **theatre** seating some 500 spectators for rituals, dances and perhaps also boxing and wrestling matches. Leading away from it, probably to link up with a main road to Knossós's port at Katsámbas, is an impressively built **royal road** with rain gutters running along the central paving.

43

GORTIS

Make an early start if you are combining this old Roman capital in one excursion with the Minoan sites of Phaistós and Agía Triáda. It is a 160-km (100-mile) round trip from Iráklion if you include a swim at Mátala. An additional 30-km (18-mile) side trip to Lendas (ancient *Lebena*) can combine a visit to the excavated Greek temple and spa with a swim at the nearby beach. For all of them, follow the signs for Phaistós from Iráklion through **chanióporta** (the western gate). After the **Pass of Vourvoulítis**, 600 m (2000 ft) above

Rich farmland of the Messará Plain contrasts with impressive Mount Ida.

sea level, the rich farmland of the **Plain of Messará** opens up before you with the Asterousia Mountains to the south east and the Libyan Sea gleaming in the distance. Nature-lovers will be so entranced by the array of wild flowers here that they may never get to Górtis. In the village of Ágia Deka (Ten Saints), the 13th-century **church** was partly built from Górtis's Roman ruins.

Stop Playing Around, Minos

Life in Minos's Royal Chambers was not all a bed of roses. The name Minos meant 'moon-being', and the ubiquitous double-headed axe was regarded as the waxing and waning moon joined back to back – symbolizing the king's power to create or destroy. But it was Minos's excessive taste for procreation which his wife Pasiphak decided to terminate. After that shocking affair that produced the Minotaur (see p.14), she found an even more dastardly way of punishing his persistent infidelity. She had a spell cast on him so that he emitted not his seed, but serpents, scorpions and centipedes, which somewhat upset his mistresses.

The **archaeological site** of Górtis is scattered over a large area. This former Roman capital, established in 67 BC, presents its temples and buildings in a charming wilderness of trees and flowers. Imagine the ancient town with a huge population of up to 300,000.

In the Roman **odeon**, incorporated in one of the walls, is the site's major find – the Dorian settlers' **Code of Laws** – carved on massive blocks of stone around 500 BC. In 17,000 letters of archaic Doric dialect, arranged in the so-called ox plow manner, 600 rows read alternately from left to right and right to left. The code lays down the laws for adultery, seduction, rape, divorce, inheritance, property mortgage and the treatment of slaves. Many historians regard the code as a vital step in the transition to modern law.

From the post-Roman city, you can see the barrel-vaulted shell of the 7th-century **Basilica of Ágios Títos**. It stands on the site where Paul's disciple Titus, first Bishop of Crete, was martyred for his over-assertive attempts at religious conversion. It was destroyed by Arab invaders in AD 825. **45**

LENDAS

Just before the church of Ágios Títos on the main road from Iráklion, a side road leads south to a lovely sheltered bay south of the Asterousia Mountains. The little town of **Lendas** occupies the site of Górtis's ancient port of **Lebena**. Both names, Greek and Phoenician, refer to the reclining lion shape of the harbour's western headland – Cape Leon.

During the 4th century BC, Lebena began to exploit the therapeutic qualities of its springwater as a highly profitable health spa. You can see today the excavated remains of the **Temple of Asclepius** (the god of healing), an oblong

Górtis's Roman odeon, with its Code of Laws, developed by an increasingly sophisticated Dorian society of the 5th century.

hostel for visitors, the stone **fountain** with recessed arch, and the **treasury** with black and red mosaic paving. The holes cut around the mosaic's sea-horse motif were the work of ancient plunderers digging for the spa's takings; loot which, in Lebena's Roman day, would far outstrip that of any modern casino. There's a secluded, sandy beach at Cape Leon.

PHAISTOS

Of all the Minoan sites in Crete, **Phaistós** (*Festós*), the King's winter palace and retreat of the priesthood, enjoys the most enchanting setting. Its ruins command a magnificent **view** over the long sweep of the Messará Plain to the Libyan Sea. The plain, flecked with olive groves and vineyards, is irrigated by the Yeropotamos River. Fresh breezes sweep the plain from Zeus's childhood playgrounds, Mount Díkti and Mount Ida, enchantingly snow-capped in spring.

Phaistós has a similar labyrinthine layout of corridors and stairways as Knossós, with a central court, but all on a lesser scale. Start from a stairway going down from the **north court**, passing on your right (outside the main palace grounds), a **theatre** with an elongated narrowing shape, like a grand piano. This has a rightful claim as the world's most ancient theatre.

Another, grander staircase leads left up to the **propylaeum**, the monumental entrance to the palace proper. Left again, across a hall where you can see the bases of its peristyle colonnade, are the **royal chambers**. East of the royal quarters are commoners' dwellings where the Phaistós Disk was found (see p.33).

From the queen's rooms, a small courtyard and corridor lead back south to the long **central court**. Most of the eastern part of the court has collapsed down the hillside, but the column bases of the western portico are all still visible. Walk to the far end to see the palace's principal **well** and then double back past what was the **sanctuary** where you will see a two-pillared crypt **47** and a hall with stone benches around its walls. Beyond the sanctuary, turn left down the **corridor of storehouses and workshops** used for metal smelting and pottery. The last house on the right has some of the huge earthenware **storage jars** used to contain oil or wine. Notice the many handles through which ropes were passed to haul the gigantic vessels around.

AGIA TRIADA

The Minoan **Royal Villa**, with a later Mycenaean village below it, is a 45-minute walk or 3-km (2-mile) drive from the palace of Phaistós. Its Minoan name remains a mystery, so it is known by that of a 14th-century Venetian church south west of the site (not to be confused with the older Byzantine church of Ágios Geórgios directly above the excavations).

Scholarly guesses as to its use include those that the site was the permanent residence of the king's relatives, a ritual centre, a prince's realm, or a

*T*he royal villa at Ágia Triáda is thought (among many theories) to have been a summer retreat.

summer hideaway for the king himself. With a splendid **view** out over the Messará Bay (in Minoan times, the sea was much closer to the villa), it is spacious but more intimate and humanly-proportioned than the palaces at Knossós or Phaistós, without a central court. Its elegance is hinted at by the fine alabaster paving.

It was here that archaeologists discovered, among many of the most valuable examples of everyday Minoan life, the *Chieftain's Cup* and the *Harvester's Vase* motifs now on display in the Archaeological Museum in Iráklion.

North of the Minoan villa is a staircase leading beyond a portico of five pillars to the later, Dorian town (dating from 14th to 12th century BC). Its centrepiece is the main **square** bordered by what were originally arcades of shops.

THE BEACHES

Diligent explorers of archaeological sites deserve a good swim. The expanding resort of **Mátala** offers a refreshing, if sometimes crowded swim in the Libyan Sea just 10 km (6 miles) south of Phaistós. The beach has fine white sand and the sea is green and gentle. You may also want to visit the famous **Mátala caves** *(spiliés Matálon)*. They have had a varied career. First hewn out of **49** the cliff by Romans for use as catacombs, they were subsequently inhabited by early Christians. After the occupying Germans used them as artillery positions during World War II, peace and love once more prevailed with the hippy troglodytes of the 1960s.

Agía Galíni, 18 km (11 miles) north west of Phaistós, is a booming tourist resort. A steep, winding road leads down to the resort, situated in a narrow crevice between high cliffs. It offers good fishing and some fine seafood restaurants.

Take a break from archaeology at Mátala with its fine beach dipping into the Libyan Sea. The famous caves provide welcome shade.

Eastern Crete

Moving away from the centre of the island's ancient Minoan civilization, you'll find the attractions are more straightforwardly hedonistic. First-rate beach resorts along the north-east coast are joined by a charming, winding corniche coast road. Indeed, the tourist industry has awarded it the ultimate accolade of the 'Cretan Riviera'.

Barely an hour's drive east from Iráklion airport, Ágios Nikólaos is the delightful main resort, but there are also smaller, less crowded spots on either side of it. Inland, you can explore exciting caves, take a hike in the Lasíthi Mountains, and wander around villages proud of their handicrafts. The south coast's main town, Ierápetra, is also becoming an increasingly popular resort.

But there is also plenty for the indefatigable archaeology buff with the wonders of the Minoan village of Gourniá (see p.55) and the spectacular palaces of Mália and Káto Zákros (see p.60).

CHERSONISOS AND MALIA

Just half an hour's drive from Iráklion, these resorts owe their popularity to long sandy beaches, among the finest in Crete, a wide range of accommodation and easy access to Minoan archaeological sites on or near the north coast.

Although thoroughly dedicated to the resort life of discos, bars and cafés, **Chersonísos** (more correctly *Limín Chersonísou*) does have vestiges of proof of its days as an ancient Hellenistic and Roman port – breakwaters, piers and quays – submerged in the harbour.

Further along the coast, **Mália** boasts a **Minoan palace** on its eastern outskirts dating from the same era as Knossós and Phaistós. In the spirit of the latter's excavations, the French archaeologists of this site avoided excessive reconstruction. You can ramble around the evocative ruins with a superb **view** over the sea. Next to the ceremonial staircase just off the south-west corner of the central court is a remarkable **51**

circular **kernós** (ritual table). Set in the limestone slab are 34 small depressions around a central hollow. One theory is that fruit seeds or grain were placed in the hollows as offerings for a good harvest. Another theory suggests it was used as a gambling game, comparable to certain board games which are played in Africa.

Nearby is the **loggia**, an elevated platform where religious rites were held. Behind it, a few steps descend to a **lustral basin** or bathroom much like the ritual *mikvah* bath of the Jews or baptismal font of early Christians.

A short walk north of the palace is the **chrysólakkos** (pit of gold), a royal burial chamber where clay idols and an exquisite gold honeybee pendant were found and are now exhibited in Iráklion's Archaeological Museum.

*W*atch the chic, sleek boats glide by at charming Ágios Nikólaos. Cretans are somewhat outnumbered here now.

AGIOS NIKOLAOS

Continuing along the National Highway to Ágios Nikólaos, you can make a detour to the charming market town of **Neápolis**, the birthplace of Petros Philargos, Pope Alexander V. The town is also known for *soumáda*, a drink made of pressed almonds that will undoubtedly cool you on a blistering hot day.

The road descends to **Ágios Nikólaos**, nestling right at the heart of the splendid *Kólpos Mirabéllou* (Bay of Mirabéllo), a beautiful resort fighting gamely to protect its natural charm against the onslaught of the package tour. The climate is dry, the winters mild, and the sports facilities excellent. You can explore this delightful bay on boat excursions from Ágios Nikólaos, or by a tortuous drive along the spectacular coast road.

To enjoy the relaxed atmosphere of the **fishing harbour** at Ágios Nikólaos, you should avoid July and August. The harbour, from which you can take cruises around Mirabéllo Bay, is bordered by restaurants **53** and shops offering, after Iráklion, the island's best selection of jewellery, ceramics and other souvenirs.

A man-made channel connects the harbour to **Lake Voulisméni**, once reputed 'bottomless' but in fact 64 m (210 ft) deep – still a surprise

*G*raceful windmills irrigating the Lasíthi Plains with subterranean supplies of water should really be known as wind pumps.

for anyone casually dropping in. From its landward cliff, which has an **aviary**, you get a great view of both lake and harbour. A *vólta* or evening promenade along the lake's quayside is almost a social obligation (see p.95).

The town's **Archaeological Museum**, on Odós Paleologou, contains an admirable collection of Minoan ceramics and gold jewellery from regional sites. Most notable are the 'teapot' and 'frying pan' vases and a distinctive libation vase, with two orifices, known as the Goddess of Myrtos.

The **kitroplateía** (municipal beach) lies south of the harbour. To the north, the smarter hotels hiding among bougainvillea, olive and palm trees, command a delightful rocky promontory in gardens dotted about with attractive modern sculptures.

The fertile plateau of the **Lasíthi Plains**, some 850 m (2800 ft) up in the Díkti Mountains offers pleasant excursions from Ágios Nikólaos. The plains are covered with apple and almond orchards and the few remaining white, cloth-sailed **windmills** which drive the irrigation system. Sadly, they are being increasingly replaced by oil-powered pumps.

ELOUNDA AND SPINALONGA ISLAND

On the western shore of Mirabéllo Bay, **Eloúnda** is a pleasant and increasingly popular resort with pebble beaches and lively restaurants clustered around its fishing harbour. On the adjacent Spinalónga peninsula, **Oloús**, a Greco-Roman settlement, is almost entirely submerged beneath the sea and makes a fas- cinating target for skin-divers. On land, an Early Christian church has been excavated to reveal a charming 4th-century dolphin mosaic.

Harbour cruises from Ágios Nikólaos or Eloúnda take you out to the arid beauty of **Spinalónga**, an island notable for its impressive 16th-century Venetian fort captured by the Turks and used briefly at the beginning of this cen-

tury as a leper colony (no danger today).

A smaller island to the south, **Agii Pandes**, serves as a nature reserve for the *agrími*, the rare Cretan ibex otherwise only to be seen in the White Mountains above the Samariá Gorge (see p.80).

GOURNIA

On a hillside above a fine natural harbour 18 km (11 miles) east of Ágios Nikólaos are the clearly defined walls and cobbled streets of the ancient Minoan town of **Gourniá**. Whereas excavators of the island's other Minoan sites concentrated on the grand palaces, American archaeologist Harriet Boyd Hawes worked from 1901 to 1904 to reveal here a whole township

You can wander among remains of houses and shops around the **agorá** (market-place) and along streets just wide enough for pedestrians and pack-animals – but not wheeled transport – leading to the palace. From the **town mosaics** in Iráklion's Archaeo-

55

E loúnda village (above) is a stylish, delightful bay. The ruins of a complete Minoan town at Gourniá (right) provide a different interest.

logical Museum, we can guess the original shape of the multi-storey houses and you can see here the external staircases that led directly to the upper living quarters last inhabited over 3000 years ago. Many people find the smallness of the dwellings quite striking, although even today the construction of Cretan villages is **56** not so very different.

PSIRA AND MOCHLOS

These two islands on the east side of the bay also have important **Minoan settlements**, parts of them submerged offshore. Of the two, tiny **Móchlos** is the easier to visit, just 150 m (490 ft) out from the very pleasant fishing village which shares its name. If you choose to swim across the channel, remember to take some shoes for clambering over the rough rocks to the ancient houses, chamber-tombs and Roman fortifications.

Divers exploring the underwater ruins should remember it is a criminal offence to remove any objects. Archaeological finds from here (and Gourniá) are shared among the museums of Ágios Nikólaos, Sitía and Iráklion.

KRITSA

Perched on a mountainside 12 km (7.5 miles) from Ágios Nikólaos, this extremely picturesque town is celebrated for its **weaving**. Along the steeply sloping streets, villagers sit in their doorways selling their shawls, rugs and table-linen.

In an olive grove on the edge of the village, the small white church of **Panagiá Kerá** (Most Holy Virgin) is a treasure trove of 14th- and 15th-century frescoes among the most admired throughout the island. The dome is decorated with four scenes from the gospel: the *Presentation of Jesus at the Temple*, the *Baptism*, the *Resurrection of Lazarus* and *Christ's Entry into Jerusalem*. On the vault of the nave you can see the *Last Supper*.

If your car can take the rough road, follow the signs leading up to **Lató**, a Doric settlement founded in the 7th century BC. The spectacular **views** from the mountains overlooking the Sea of Crete are worth the 45-minute walk.

DIKTAEAN CAVE

Take your best walking shoes, warm sweater and a pocket torch to explore the cavernous childhood home of Zeus, **Diktéon Ántron**, 1025 m (3360 ft) above sea level. The entrance is a 20-minute walk west of the village of **Psichró**, **57**

75 km (47 miles) from Ágios Nikólaos via Neápolis.

The visit is an adventure, a steep and tricky passage 60 m (200 ft) down to a cave that is damp, slippery and dimly lit – just the way caves should be. The discovery here of stone altars and bronze votive offerings, including the Minoan double-axe, (now in Iráklion's Archaeological Museum) revealed the cave as an important sanctuary during the Minoan era. The impressive stalagmites and stalactites you will see here took on, in the flickering light of pilgrims' lamps, the shape of divinities. One is still known as the Cloak of Zeus.

Just outside the charming little resort of Istro, a winding road climbs along the eastern edge of the Díkti Mountains to the spectacularly situated village of **Kalamáfka**.

On the approach to the town, you will be afforded the unusual pleasure of being able to look down simultaneously

---

Tough Baby

Cretan tour-operators and scholars of Greek mythology argue about whether the Diktaean Cave or the one on Mount Ida was Zeus's birthplace. Another version, popular with Peloponnesian tour-operators, suggests Zeus was in fact born on Mount Lycaeon, in the heart of the Peloponnese.

His mother, Rhea, sent him off to Crete, safe from his father's plan to eat him. Because of a prophecy that he would be dethroned by one of his offspring, Cronos, Lord of the Titans, had already devoured his other five children. When he came looking for Zeus, Rhea fooled him with a stone wrapped in swaddling clothes, which he promptly swallowed.

Thereafter, Zeus grew up in the Diktaean Cave, weaned on goat's milk and good Cretan honey. He spent his teens with shepherds on Mount Ida. When he was big enough, he went off and struck his father with a thunderbolt. Such is life in the hands of the gods.

on both the Sea of Crete to the north and south to the Libyan Sea.

If you are heading for the south coast resort of Ierápetra, the landscape, especially with the wild flowers in spring, make this much more rewarding than the shorter, direct route further east.

IERAPETRA

Just east of Gourniá, a modern highway follows the ancient carriageway which crosses the island at its narrowest point, just 14 km (9 miles) wide, to the resort which claims to be Europe's southernmost town – Africa is just 300 km (187 miles) away. Certainly it is the only large town on Crete's south coast and its mild climate and year-round supply of fresh fruit and vegetables make it an attractive spot, even (or especially) in winter when the crowds have diminished. It has a good **beach**, and a **Venetian fort**, dating back to the 13th century, adds a certain character to the pleasant fishing harbour.

In summer, boats go out to the little island of **Gaidouronísi** for a quieter swim and meal in the taverna.

SITIA

The heady drive from Ágios Nikólaos to the eastern end of the island winds along a mountain road with plunging views over the sea. This is the corniche they call the Cretan Riviera. Between orchards and olive groves, it passes white villages perched precariously on steep slopes, clearly ready to topple into the ravine at the first hint of an earthquake.

A frequent victim of earthquakes, the old Venetian port of **Sitía** was much plundered by the Turkish pirate Barbarossa and abandoned for two centuries after its destruction in 1651. It has since recovered to become a lively resort and **port** for boats coming from Ágios Nikólaos.

The **Venetian fortress** makes a handsome setting for summer concerts and plays. The beaches are good, the restaurants very good. Visit **59** the **Archaeological Museum** before going to the Minoan palace of Káto Zákros, from where many of the most recent finds, notably a reconstituted Minoan wine-press, have been brought (see below).

East of Sitía, a turn-off and a short, rough road leads to the **Moní Toploú** (Touplou Monastery), a 14th-century edifice, later fortified by the Venetians. Its somewhat irreligious Turkish name means 'cannon', referring to the Venetian artillery which (sadly unsuccessfully) attempted to defend it in 1645. The most important of the many icons, by Ioánnis Kornáros, comprises 60 scenes entitled *Lord, Thou Art Great* (1770), hallowed as a masterpiece of art from the Byzantine era.

Further east, the delightful beach at **Váï** attracts swarms of bathers in summer, drawn by the fame of its fine sand, translucent green waters and above all the groves of palm trees (Váï means 'palm'). The trees are said to have grown from date stones spat out by Arab invaders.

KATO ZAKROS

The fourth great Minoan palace lies at the farthest south-eastern point of the island. The road from Sitía to Káto Zákros crosses a high plateau with views across a vast gorge and Karoubes Bay before winding through banana plantations down to the sea and a delightful little beach with pleasant tavernas. Linked to its harbour by a stone-paved road, the **Minoan palace** was enriched by the town's flourishing sea trade with Egypt and the Middle East. Its strategic position, facing the Orient, also made it the principal naval base for the defence of the island.

Originally discovered by a British archaeologist in 1901, the work for the palace excavations was entirely financed by a wealthy American couple with a strong interest in art and archaeology.

Typically Cretan, Sitía is a good spot from where to take excursions to sites of interest.

The Zákros palace layout is similar to those at Knossós, Phaistós and Mália, with the **shrine** and **ritual bath** to the west and **royal apartments** to the east of the central court. The shrine's **treasury** was the only one to be found unplundered, revealing a magnificent collection of ivory and bronze, ornate chalices and vases, now on display at the Sitía Archaeological Museum. Behind the royal apartments is the rectangular **Hall of the Cistern** with steps leading down to a circular underground pool 7 m (22 ft) wide, unique among the Minoan palaces, that has variously been interpreted as the king's swimming pool, a royal aquarium or a ceremonial pool for a sacred boat.

This palace also has the unusual distinction of a well-defined **kitchen** area north of the central court. Climb up to the ancient town area above the palace for a good view over the whole site.

*L*ong white stretches of sand and warm blue seas at Váï are very welcome after visiting Káto Zákros and the Toploú Monastery.

Western Crete

This quieter end of the island affords a great opportunity to explore small inland villages, sleepy fishing ports and the secluded beaches of the southwest coast. In addition, Réthimnon and Chaniá are two popular resorts with good beaches, plenty of watersports facilities and some colourful reminders of their Venetian and Turkish past.

Ramblers with a taste for the great outdoors head for Zeus's cave on *Óros Idi* (Mount Ida) and the Samariá and Imbros gorges in the White Mountains.

RETHIMNON

Well-established tourist facilities are now being enhanced by a steady programme of restoration in the attractive old quarters of Réthimnon's Venetian heyday and the Turkish years.

On an island where, in the absence of a university, most intellectuals head for Athens, Réthimnon remains a haven for Cretan artists and writers. Outside the peak tourist season, they gather in the old cafés away from the seafront. Summer arts festivals are held in and around the old fort, with an emphasis on Renaissance music and theatre which

---

Long Past Their Shelf Time

Zákros was the last of the four Minoan palaces to be unearthed, in 1961, by Professor Nikoláos Pláton, who made some outstanding discoveries. Not only was the treasury untouched, yielding much of the island's best-preserved bronze and stoneware, but the palace kitchen came with an almost complete set of utensils. Most astounding of all, in a ritual well-chamber still filled with springwater, was a votive-cup of olives, 3000 years old but preserved as if they had just been picked. As soon as they were exposed to the air, they disintegrated.

flourished here during the Venetian era.

To plunge into the historic dual Venetian and Turkish ambiance of the **old town**, park your car by the public gardens (scene of the Cretan Wine Festival in July – see p.97) and pass under the Venetian arched gateway, **Porta Cuora**, to discover a town that still has the street plan of its Renaissance origins. A minaret and domes have turned the church of Santa Maria into the **Djamí ton Neranzión** (Mosque of Neranzies).

You get a fine view of the city from the balcony where once the muezzin called the faithful to prayer. At the other end of Platía Petiháki, beyond the square's palm trees, the **Rimondi Fountain** with its Venetian lions crowning the Corinthian columns has, confusingly, a Turkish dome.

East of the square on Odós Arkádiu, the elegant **loggia** – similar to the one reconstructed in Iráklion – served as a clubhouse for Venetian gentlemen. South along Odós Arkádiu, the **old houses**, most of them converted into shops, offer an enchanting combination of Venetian stone façades with vaulted ground floors beneath overhanging wooden balconies added by the Turks. Peep in at the pebbled courtyards with their stone staircases to the upper living quarters.

Following the long sandy beach curving lazily around the bay towards the old harbour, the **Venizélou Promenade** is lined with outdoor cafés, restaurants and shops. This is the natural venue for morning souvenir shopping and Réthimnon's evening stroll, the *vólta* (see also p.95). Liveliest gathering place for a seafood supper is the tiny Venetian harbour itself, sheltering a few small sailing vessels and fishing boats watched over by the old lighthouse on the jetty.

The formidable 16th-century Venetian **Fortétza** (fortress), can be reached by an ancient stairway from Odós Melissinoú. It dominates the town's western promontory and its outer wall is worth a visit for the fine view back over the city and harbour.

64

A Selection of Hotels and Restaurants on Crete

Recommended Hotels

The following hotels are listed alphabetically in three price categories, grouped in seven resort areas: Iráklion, Chersonísos, Ágios Nikólaos/Eloúnda, Sitía, Ierápetra, Réthimnon and Chaniá. Prices will of course vary according to season and unpredictable inflation. For booking directly with the hotel, we have included telephone and, wherever possible, fax numbers.

All have air-conditioning and restaurant unless otherwise stated. As a basic guide to room prices, we have used the following symbols (double room with bath, including breakfast):

I	below 6000
II	6000-10,000
III	above 10,000 drachmas

IRAKLION

Agapi Beach　　III
Amoudari (Iráklion region).
Tel. (081) 250 502,
fax (081) 258 731.
Luxury resort hotel with private beach 15 minutes west of Iráklion. 203 rooms and bungalows, boutiques, tennis, swimming pool and other sports facilities.

Arina Sand　　II
Hani Kokkini (Iráklion region).
Tel. (081) 761 354,
fax (081) 761 179.

Modern hotel 20 minutes from Iráklion. 233 rooms, private beach, tennis, swimming pool.

Astoria　　II
Platía Eleftherías, Iráklion.
Tel. (081) 229 012.
Old-established hotel a stone's throw from the Archaeological Museum. 120 rooms.

Galaxy　　II
Dimokrátias Avenue 67,
Iráklion. Tel. 232 157.
Conveniently located on main road to Knossós, 140 rooms open all year, swimming pool, sauna, terraced garden.

Idi   I
Zaros (Iráklion region).
Tel. (30.894) 31302.
In the foothills of Mount Ida, ideal for mountain excursions. 32 rooms, swimming pool.

CHERSONISOS

Antinoös   II
Limín Chersonísos.
Tel. (0897) 23142.
Unusually tasteful, 29 individually designed rooms, two minutes east of town.

Creta Maris   III
Limín Chersonísos.
Tel. (0897) 22115.
Giant modern hotel complex. 516 rooms, small private beach, two minutes from public beach, tennis, swimming pool and live music entertainment.

Cretan Village   III
Limín Chersonísos.
Tel. (0897) 22996.
Traditional Cretan-style houses, 228 rooms.

AGIOS NIKOLAOS/ ELOUNDA

Ariadne Beach   I
Ágios Nikólaos.
Tel. (0841) 22741,
fax (0841) 22005.
Pretty setting in landscaped gardens with private beach, 76 rooms and bungalows, swimming pool and good sports facilities.

Astir Palace   III
Eloúnda.
Tel. (0841) 41580,
fax (0841) 41783.
Luxury resort hotel beautifully situated on Mirabéllo Bay. 297 rooms, tennis, private sandy beach, two swimming pools and other sports facilities, live music entertainment.

Eloúnda Beach   III
Eloúnda.
Tel. (0841) 41412,
fax (0841) 41373.
Large, luxurious and modern hotel in grand style 7 kms (4 miles) from the town. 301 rooms, tennis, private beach, **67**

swimming pool and other sports facilities.

Eloúnda Island Villas II

Eloúnda.
Tel. (0841) 41274.
On Spinalónga Island, 15 apartments, tennis courts, small beach.

Minos Beach III

Ágios Nikólaos.
Tel. (0841) 22345,
fax (0841) 22548.
Luxurious, hospitable resort hotel in handsomely landscaped gardens with private beach, tennis, swimming pool, gift shops, live music entertainment.

SITIA

El Greco I

Sitía. Tel. (0843) 23133.
In quiet central location. 15 rooms, open all year.

Elysee I

Karamánlis Street 14, Sitía.
Tel (0843) 22312.

Seafront location, friendly, family hotel. 24 rooms.

Kappa Crete II

Karamánlis Street, Sitía.
Tel (0843) 28821.
Modern beach hotel. 162 rooms, tennis, swimming pool and other sports facilities, live music entertainment.

Sunwing III/II/I

Makrigiálos, Sitía.
Tel. (0843) 51621
fax (0843) 51626.
Huge resort complex. 371 rooms and apartments. Private beach, tennis, swimming pool.

Váï I

Itanou-Dimokritou, Sitía.
Tel. (0843) 22528.
Small and modern, 44 rooms, five minutes from the beach.

IERAPETRA

Ferma Beach II

Ferma (Ierápetra region).
Tel. (0842) 61352,
fax (0842) 61416.
156 rooms and bungalows 9 kms (6 miles) east of Ierápetra.

Private beach, tennis, swimming pool and live music entertainment.

Petra Mare III
Ierápetra. Tel. (0842) 23341, fax (0842) 23350.
On eastern outskirts of town, large resort complex, 219 rooms, private beach, swimming pool, live music entertainment.

RETHIMNON

Creta Star II
Stavromenos (Réthimnon region).
Tel. (0831) 71812, fax (0831) 71791
Luxury resort complex. 324 rooms. tennis, private beach, swimming pool and other sports facilities.

Fortezza II
Melissinoú Street 16, Réthimnon.
Tel. (0831) 21551, fax (0831) 20073.
Modern hotel, 54 rooms, nicely located in old town, three minutes from beach, tennis, swimming pool.

Rithymna Beach III
Adelianos Kambos, Réthimnon.
Tel. (0831) 29491.
Mammoth resort complex. 556 rooms and bungalows, 7 kms (4 miles) from town, private beach, swimming pool.

CHANIA

Amphora II
Parodos Theotokopoúlos 20, Chaniá.
Tel. (0821) 42998.
Charming old medieval mansion – the prettiest building on the harbour front. 14 rooms, 10 minutes from beach, open all year.

Casa Delfino III
Theofanous 9, Paleo Poli, Chaniá.
Tel. (0821) 42613.
Exquisite 17th-century Venetian mansion, 12 furnished studios.

Porto Veneziano II
Enetikos Limín, Chaniá.
Tel. (0821) 29311.
Near Venetian harbour, 63 rooms, 10 minutes from beach. **69**

Recommended Restaurants

The following choices concentrate on restaurants and tavernas serving local cuisine rather than the easy-to-find 'international' places, pizzerias and other fast-food outlets.

Apart from a few pretentious establishments and luxury hotel-restaurants (none of which we have included here), average meal prices (starter, main course and dessert) range from around 1500-2000 drachmas per person (drinks will increase the bill further). We note those significantly more expensive, but otherwise the following symbols rate cuisine, ambience and service:

I	fair
II	good
III	excellent

Some restaurants close one day a week, which may vary in and out of season, so telephone first to confirm. Many restaurants and tavernas are open only for dinner.

IRAKLION

Galera **II**

Knossoú St, Iráklion.
Tel. (081) 210 491.

Good quality seafood, above-average prices.

Gerakas **II**

Dimokrátias St 43,
Nea Alikarnásos.
Tel. (081) 244 854.

In suburban taverna east of Iráklion, first-class fresh fish.

Minos **I**

Dedalou St 10, Iráklion.
Tel. (081) 281 263.
Cretan specialities in traditional Greek taverna.

Petousis **III**

Gazi. Tel. (081) 821 376.
Taverna serving first-class mezédes and home-made Cretan desserts.

Vardia **I**

The Harbour.
Tel. (081) 223 736.

Friendly atmosphere on waterfront – good mezédes.

AGIOS NIKOLAOS

Cretan Restaurant   II
Koundourou St, Ágios Nikólaos.
Tel. (0841) 31726.

Elegant harbourside restaurant serving both Greek specialities and international cuisine, good but expensive.

Life is Beautiful   II
Pasifais St, Ágios Nikólaos.
Tel. (0841) 23478.

Local artists favour this charming old house serving traditional Greek food accompanied by jazz music.

Mbokhos   I
Solomou St, Ágios Nikólaos.
Tel. (0841) 23890.

Lakeside taverna specializing in grills and seafood. Popular with the locals.

ELOUNDA

Manolis   II
Plaka, Eloúnda.
Tel. (0841) 41289.
Fine fresh fish, friendly service, with waterfront terrace view of Spinalónga Island.

Medusa   I
Ágios Nikólaos-Eloúnda Road.
Tel. (0841) 41698.
Fish tavern with terrace overlooking the sea.

Olondi   I
The Harbour, Eloúnda.
Tel. (0841) 41040.
Friendly waterfront restaurant serving grills and seafood.

SITIA

Kolios   II
Venizelos St 167, Sitía.
Tel. (0843) 28607.
Fresh fish, Greek specialities and good wine list.

Mixos   II
Vitzentzi Kornaro St 117, Sitía.
Tel. (0843) 22416.

Barbecue grills, lamb, stuffed calamari in tavern popular with local citizens.

Taverna I. Anesis   I
Káto Zákros (Sitía region).
Tel (0843) 26738.
Beachfront taverna, Greek specialities and seafood.

RETHIMNON

Alana   II
Salaminos St 11, Réthimnon.
Tel. (0831) 27737.
Good traditional cooking in charming courtyard.

George   I
Fortezza, Réthimnon.
Tel. (0831) 21163.
Near Archaeological Museum, terraced taverna offering fish and grills.

Mouragio   I
The Harbour, Réthimnon. Tel.
(0831) 26475.
Waterfront fish taverna.

Stratidakis   I
Spili (Réthimnon region).
Tel. (0831) 27986.

Traditional country cuisine in pretty village setting.

CHANIA

Kali Kardia   I
Kondilaki St 31, Chaniá.
Tel (0831) 56354.
Traditional taverna in old Evréïka (Jewish) quarter, good desserts.

Marco Polo   III
Akti Tobazi, Chaniá.
No telephone.
Superb fresh fish near harbour behind Turkish mosque, slightly above average prices, but worth it.

Ombros Ialos   I
Chóra Sfakíon,
(Chaniá region).
Tel. (0825) 91204.
Cheerful taverna in main square

Tamam   II
Sambelu St 49, Chaniá.
No telephone.
In the cellar of an old Turkish baths, popular with artists and writers.

*R*éthimnon's lazy harbour, framed by picturesque Venetian houses, has been a source of inspiration for many artists and writers.

These walls once enclosed warehouses, artillery placements, a garrison, church and hospital. The most important of the surviving buildings are part of the **governor's residence**, near the main gate, and the imposing ruin of **Sultan Ibrahim Mosque**, built on the site of the Venetians' cathedral.

The town's **Archaeological Museum**, housed in a Venetian prison near the fort, displays prehistoric clay sarcophagi, tools of bone and obsidian, Bronze Age jewellery, Minoan and Dorian stone and clay figurines, and ritual artefacts from Zeus's Idaian Cave. A small **Folk Art Museum** (28 Odós Messolonghí) has a good collection of traditional weaving, jewellery, basketry, utensils and tools.

73

MONASTERY OF ARKADI

A 45-minute drive south east of Réthimnon (via Platánias) takes you up along a spectacular gorge to one of the most revered sites of Crete's resistance to Turkish occupation.

Perched on a rugged mountainside, in 1866 the 16th-century **Moní Arkadíou** became an armed bastion of revolt, with hundreds of villagers taking refuge within. Rather than surrender to besieging Turkish troops, Abbot Gabriel waited for them to break into the monastery and then blew up the gunpowder magazine, killing hundreds of Turkish soldiers as well as nearly a thousand villagers. His action forever symbolized the Cretan motto 'Freedom or death'.

The monastery has since been restored in an attempt to recapture something of the ornate Venetian style. Notice that the refectory is still pockmarked with bullet holes from the Turkish siege. A **museum** preserves relics of the suicidal massacre with an **ossuary** displaying the victims' bones.

In somewhat gruesome exaltation of suffering, the people of Arkádi and Réthimnon celebrate the November 9 anniversary of this supreme act of faith with solemn memorial services, although they are quickly followed up with festive fireworks, music and dancing.

MOUNT IDA AND THE IDAIAN CAVE

Mount Ida is hallowed in Greek mythology as one of the childhood homes of Zeus. It was easy for him. He was whisked up here on a cloud. For us ordinary mortals, the mountain road to his Idaian Cave is a rough but manageable drive with a short walk from the carpark – the old mystic mathematician Pythagoras made the whole pilgrimage on foot. The scenery alone makes the trip worthwhile. (Before you set out, check if it is open with

A surprisingly elaborate façade heralds the brave, remote Arkádi Monastery.

Réthimnon's tourist office as it sometimes closes due to archaeological excavations.)

Just beyond **Anógia**, the mountain road turns off south up to Mount Ida, more commonly known locally as **Psilorítis**, 'the high one', in fact Crete's highest one at 2456 m (8055 ft). If you want to climb all the way to the top (nine hours there and back), take a guide with you from Anógia and plan to spend the night so that you can witness the sunrise. On the summit, there is a **chapel** for shelter and meditation. The mountain is snow-capped till late spring, but in May and June – whether you drive or hike – the wild flowers along the route are a sheer joy, with a veritable explosion of colour when you get to the **Pediáda tis Nídas** (Plain of Nída) standing at 1400 m (4600 ft).

Whatever the competing claims of the Diktaean Cave (see p.57), the Greeks certainly treated the **cave** on Mount Ida as a sanctuary. It was believed that King Minos came here every seven years to get a new **75** batch of laws from Zeus, making Ida a kind of Mount Sinai. Italian excavators found votive offerings, gold jewellery, precious gems, ceremonial bronze shields and a bronze drum, all now on display in the museums of Iráklion and Réthimnon.

AMARI VALLEY

This excursion along the western slopes of Mount Ida makes a beautiful round-trip any time of year but is most bewitching in springtime. Starting east of Réthimnon, the **Amari** road winds up through ancient olive groves and meadows filled with wild red tulips, lupins and tiny irises. Art-lovers will appreciate, too, the frescoes of the Byzantine churches (equip yourself with a pocket-torch).

After Apostoli, take the valley's left fork uphill to **Thronos**. Against the spectacular backdrop of Mount Ida, the little 14th-century **Panagia chapel** stands on a terrace still bearing traces of mosaics from an Early Christian basilica from the 4th century BC.

Inside the chapel are **frescoes** revealing the Venetian contribution of dramatic realism to the more formal Byzantine tradition.

On the south side of town, a signpost points you to the acropolis of the ancient Greek town of **Sybrita**, well worth the easy 15-minute climb for the **view** and, in springtime, the meadows carpeted with wild flowers on the way.

At the Asomaton Monastery, with a proud history of Cretan resistance to the Turks and now a tranquil agricultural college, the Amari road turns right to Monastiraki where the **church of Arkhistratigos** has a fine fresco of the *Assumption of the Virgin*. **Amari** itself boasts the island's oldest frescoes (1225) in the **chapel of St Anna**, beautifully situated surrounded by woods. You will find other noteworthy frescoes in the churches of Opsigias and Lampiotes.

Return to Asomaton Monastery to take the main valley road to **Vizari**. On the west side of the village, green signposts take you out into the country to the remains of an **Early Christian basilica** of the 6th century. Continue on down just past Fourfouras for a view across the Messará Plain to the Libyan Sea before doubling back via **Platanía** where the Panagía church has some 15th-century frescoes.

CHANIA

Like Réthimnon, Chaniá makes an agreeable mixture of its Venetian and Turkish influences in buildings standing on the site of the Minoan city of Kydonía. To keep the charm intact, make a conscious effort to ignore the garish modern neighbourhoods.

The grand loop of the **Venetian Harbour** is without doubt the town's most outstanding feature. Indeed, viewed at sunset from the lighthouse at the end of the long breakwater of golden stone, the lights of the shops, cafés and tavernas make up one of the most enchanting images on the whole island. At the west end of the loop is the **Firkás**, a restored section

of the Venetian ramparts, housing the **Naftikó Mousío** (Naval Museum) with ship models from ancient Greek times to a 20th-century submarine, and scenes of key episodes in Greek naval history. Facing it across the harbour is the **Djamí ton Genissarión** (Mosque of the Janissaries), the oldest of Chaniá's Turkish buildings (1645), now housing the Tourist Information Centre.

Ancient Kydonía is buried beneath the **Kastélli quarter** behind the mosque. Several antiquities came to light after the bombardments of World War II and, as you will see by the occasional excavated pit or trench around **Platía Ágia Ekateríni**, archaeologists still potter around, until they are chased away by new builders.

The neighbouring **Splánzia quarter** to the east is dominated on the waterfront by the **arsenali**, seven of the original 17 barrel-vaulted hangars where the Venetians built and repaired their ships. Behind them you can walk back to the Orthodox **Church of Ágios 77**

Nikólaos, ecumenically sporting a Venetian Catholic belltower and Turkish Moslem minaret.

In the Turkish **Topanás quarter** behind the Firkás, explore the narrow lanes where the houses have Venetian stone façades with wooden upper storeys added by the Turks, a Venetian city gate and a Turkish well. Along Odós Theotokopoúlou, you will find good local craftware.

For a wide range of leather goods, including handmade shoes and boots, head for Odós Skridlof in the former Jewish **Evréïka quarter**.

A covered market-place, **Dimotikí Agorá**, dominates the centre of town. Bustling but clean and efficient, the stalls overflowing with Cretan fruit and vegetables show just how fertile an island it is. Buy the olives, tomatoes, salad and goat's cheese here for a picnic.

Housed in the Venetian monastery church of St Francis in Evréïka, the **Archeológiko Mousío** (Archaeological Museum) displays, in addition to some interesting Stone Age sculpture and ceramics, important recent finds from the Kastélli excavations showing the origins of Kydonía. A major exhibit among these finds is the depiction of the ancient town known as the *Master Impression*.

Away from the city centre, at Odós Sfakianáki 20, the **Historical Museum** offers a keen insight into the pungent flavour of modern Greek and more especially Cretan patriotism. It exhibits the earnest, flashing-eyed portraits of rebel

*F*ew would guess at Chaniá's violent past from its beautiful, serene harbourfront of today.

chiefs throughout the struggles for independence and documents the fierce resistance to Turks and Germans. A special room dedicated to the career of Chaniá's most illustrious son, Greek Prime Minister, Elefthérios Venizélos.

AKROTIRI

The peninsula east of Chaniá embraces the spectacular land-locked harbour of **Kólpos Soúdas** (Soúda Bay) which serves Chaniá-bound passengers on the overnight ferry from Piraeus. The cafés in Soúda's little squares are filled with sailors, since the harbour is also a naval base for the Greek navy and its NATO allies. The long green slope at the head of the bay is the **British War Cemetery** for British and Commonwealth soldiers killed in Crete during World War II.

First stop is the hill of **Profítis Ilías**, scene of the Cretan insurgents' heroic resistance to the Turks in 1897. Beside the impressive tomb of Greek Prime Minister Elef-

thérios Venizélos, you get a panoramic **view** over the Gulf of Chaniá.

Drive through the peninsula's cheerful countryside, bright with wild flowers in springtime, to visit three monasteries. The fine 17th-century monastery of **Agía Triáda** (Holy Trinity), with its nest of domes, is a major pilgrimage centre, but tourist visitors are welcomed. A few kilometres further (one hour's walk) is the older and more isolated **Moní Gouvernétou**. Another bracing one-hour hike takes you down to the abandoned monastery of **Katholikó** built beside a bridge at the foot of the cliffs. The caves were inhabited by pagan and Christian hermits, with stalagmites on which they hung their clothes.

SAMARIA GORGE

There are two ways to tackle the hike to the spectacular **Farági Samariás** (Samariá Gorge). Hardy ramblers drive or take the bus from Chaniá to Omalós, 42 km (26 miles) and take the all-day hike – 18 km

(11 miles) – down to the sea at Agía Rouméli. There, a boat brings them to the bus (or pre-arranged taxi) at Chóra Sfakíon for the return to Chaniá. The more easygoing approach is to drive directly to Chóra Sfakíon and take the boat to Agía Rouméli. Then explore just the bottom of the gorge in the early morning (before the day-hikers reach it) and sail back to your return transport at Chóra Sfakíon.

If you are hiking right through the gorge, **Omalós** is a good place to have breakfast at one of the cafés, and to stock up with picnic goods. You will find springs, drinking troughs and a couple of WCs down in the gorge. Take along a bottle of water all the same, and a hat, as the sun beats down relentlessly and there is little shade. You will also need a pair of good walking shoes for the rocky path.

The descent to the gorge begins with a **xilóskalon** (wooden staircase – also the name of the bus terminus). Park wardens give you a ticket (no charge) to be given up at the other end as a means of checking that no one is stranded in the gorge at the end of the day.

With the huge rock wall of **Mount Gingilos** towering on your right, the staircase dwindles into a stone path dropping sharply away 1000 m (3280 ft) to the upper gorge bed in the first couple of kilometres. Take it easy and keep to the designated path. The route is considerably less steep once you reach the **chapel of Ágios Nikólaos** tucked away among majestic cypresses and pines to your right. Among the blues, greens and greys of the rocks, the pools are invitingly cool and clear, but take heed of the warning that swimming is strictly forbidden.

The hamlet of **Samariá** and the Venetian **church of Ossia Maria** (Mary's Bones) mark the halfway point. Beyond it is the gorge's narrowest point, the famous **Sideróportes** (Iron Gates) hemmed in on either side by rock walls 300 m (1000 ft) high. From here, the gorge opens up in its approach to the sea. **81**

*T*he hardy hiker is soon sorted from the casual tourist once down in the Samariá Gorge.

At **Agía Rouméli**, the Libyan Sea awaits you for a relaxing swim. After your dip, visit the **church of Panagía**, built over an ancient temple to Apollo, whose black, white and red mosaic floor can still be seen in the forecourt.

IMBROS GORGE

This hike is favoured by those seeking to avoid the mob scene that can spoil Samariá in high season. It also offers a gentler descent than Samariá but with equally spectacular scenery, notable for its wild flowers, especially the lovely purple blooms of Jerusalem sage. A 90-minute bus ride on the deliciously hair-raising Chaniá to Chóra Sfakíon road brings you to the village of **Imbros**. From here, you can hike right through the gorge almost to the sea – 11 km (7 miles) – in about five to six hours. If you are driving, stop off at **Vríses** to sample what connoisseurs consider to be the best yoghurt on the island, At the end of the village of Imbros, take a sharp left turn down to the dried-up riverbed and then turn right towards the sea.

The gorge ends at the village of Kommitades. Take the bus down to **Chóra Sfakíon**, where you can plunge in for a refreshing swim and indulge in the many seafood restaurants bordering the harbour.

The people of the region – the Sfakiots – are renowned throughout Greece for their courageous deeds in the battles for independence. Some 15 km (9 miles) east of the town is the stark silhouette of the massive 14th-century Venetian fortress of **Frangokástello**. Its fine, sandy beach is accessible by boat or road. At dawn in mid-May, climatic conditions create an eerie mist around the castle's four great towers and Cretans see the ghosts of Sfakiots who died defending the fort against the Turks.

THE WESTERN BEACHES

West of Chaniá, the facilities for watersports or plain lazing on the beach vary from the sophisticated to the very simple. On the north coast are the elaborate modern resort complex of **Máleme** and long sandy beaches of **Kastélli Kissámou**. On the west coast is the splendid long curving bay of **Falásarna**. This important trade port in the 4th century BC offers a bonus for those interested in archaeology with its excavated remains scattered over the cliffs. Down the coast, visit the delightful secluded fishing village of **Sfinári** and take a dip from its pebbled beach. Further south is the **Moní Chrisoskalítissa** (Chrisoskalítissa Convent) – inquire at the café for the keys to see the church frescoes.

On the south coast, **Paleochóra** is a busy little port with plenty of accommodation and lively taverns. It is a good base from which to take excursions to the coral pink beaches of the **Elafonísi islands**. Or head further south to the island of **Gávdos**, which local folklore and classical scholars have identified as the island where Odysseus dallied with Calypso while his poor wife Penelope patiently weaved and unravelled her tapestry.

83

What to Do

Modern visitors to Crete have a lesson to learn from the island's ancient Minoan civilization. Cretans excel in the arts – or at least in the architecture, sculpture and painting they have bequeathed us – without losing their taste for fun and games. There is more to this island than just sight-seeing and soaking up the sun. Moreover, siestas are particularly enjoyable if you actually do something in between.

Not surprisingly, most of the activities on the island have an uncanny knack of capturing the spirit of ancient Greece and its subsequent Venetian and Turkish conquerors. The real bargains in shopping are the products of the island's authentic folk arts. The best jewellery renews ancient designs. If most of the sports are resolutely modern – difficult to imagine Theseus waterskiing after his bout with the Minotaur – sailing across Mirabéllo Bay or along the south coast to Chóra Sfakíon can still evoke a miniature Odyssey.

Entertainment is not only an over-amplified *bouzoúki* cassette, it can also be Renaissance Italian Chamber music under the stars at Réthimnon. The year-round town and village festivals maintain a link between the ancient customs of pagan carnivals and the more solemn religious processions of the Orthodox Church.

Opening Hours

Generally, hours are 8.30 a.m. to 1.30 p.m. and 5.30 to 8.30 p.m. Tuesday, Thursday and Friday; 8.30 a.m. to 2 p.m. Monday, Wednesday and Saturday. Some shops may 'break' these rules and stay open later if, for instance, at Ágios Nikólaos a cruise-ship has docked with big-spending customers staying overnight.

*B*right and colourful hand-made wall-hangings, rugs and shoulder bags (tagária or voúrgia) entice at many a shop entrance.

SHOPPING

Walk into the bazaar or market with your eyes wide open and you will soon sift the wheat from the chaff. Rugs, pottery, furs, gold and silver jewellery, moderate or expensive, are the bargains to look for.

Antiques

Amateur and professional archaeologists can no longer carry off their chance findings. Anything that predates Greek independence in 1821 is considered an antique and must have an export permit which **85** is practically impossible to acquire for anything truly ancient. Customs officials have a keen eye open for the big pieces, while smaller removable items like coins and terracotta or bronze figurines are probably fake anyway. From the Byzantine era, if you are in the market for icons (easily faked, too), you may find reputable dealers in Iráklion. Those content with good replicas or modern icons in a traditional style will find the best bargains in the museum shops and monasteries.

Clothes and Leatherware

Unless you are determined to go native, the folk look suits Greek people much better. Local weavers do produce brightly coloured jerseys, capes and smocks for both men and women. At best, try a fisherman's sweater, a pair of sandals or boots, still handmade in villages in the western half of the island.

Folk Art

Craftwork is not all mass produced in factories. Traditional handmade creations by artisans maintain a high standard and a remarkably low price. Iráklion and the major resorts have pottery, wood carving, fabrics, lace and embroidery from all over the island. It is a good idea to look at the range – and price – of goods there and compare them with what you might find in mountain villages like Kritsá or Anógia.

Before buying, take a look at the government-sponsored display in Réthimnon (in the Tourist Information Centre

Cane and wicker, colourful or natural, make excellent inexpensive souvenirs.

building on the seafront) which offers a representative display of craftwork from all over the island. Otherwise, the historical and folk art museums (Iráklion, Réthimnon and Chaniá) are good places to check out the best of local production without being hassled by shopkeepers.

Jewellery

The style of gold and silver jewellery is often dictated by ancient history rather than

Nibbling As You Go

When you go walking through town, even if it is only to window shop, take along a bag. As you pass a market or corner grocer, you will not be able to resist the olives, pickles, dried meat and fish, cracked wheat and every other imaginable grain. Nor the nuts, beans, dried fruit (figs, raisins and apricots), ouzo-drenched fig cake wrapped in vine leaves, spices, chocolate, honey and yoghurt.

Here is a short shopping list:

almonds	**amìgdala**
apricots	**verìkoka**
capers	**kapàri**
cracked wheat	**pligoùri**
dates	**chourmàs**
figs	**sika**
honey	**mèli**
olives	**eliès**
peaches	**rodàkina**
peanuts	**fistìkia aràpika**
pistachios	**fistikia eginis**
raisins	**stafida sultanina**
walnuts	**karidia**

more recent regional traditions. Designers have moved beyond the time-honoured lacy, fine, silver filigree to draw inspiration from the great museum collections. Difficult to improve on the necklaces, bracelets, rings and earrings of Knossós, however. Just as timeless are the ancient designs for plates, bowls and chalices. But you will also find more modern designs, executed with equally admirable workmanship.

Gold and silver are sold by weight, with a relatively small fraction of the cost added for workmanship and creativity. You will find the best selection at shops in Iráklion (near the museum) and Ágios Nikólaos (around the harbour).

Pottery

Ancient art is not dead. Most of the major north coast towns produce attractive replicas of Minoan and geometrically patterned vases. The best range is at Iráklion's pottery factories, where you can buy direct or sometimes negotiate a better price at the shops near the

Archaeological Museum. At Ágios Nikólaos, try the shops around the port. Smaller shops copy famous museum models, hand-painted on the premises. They will ship fragile goods for you.

Souvenirs

Most souvenirs are so marvellously awful as to demand your immediate attention. Shopkeepers go out of their way to warn you, however, with a sign 'Greek Art', with which they hope to enhance the item with an ancient seal of quality.

Although you can find good certified 'museum copies' of classical Greek statues and fine handmade dolls in traditional costume, the amount of kitsch souvenirs knows no bounds. Miniature white Corinthian columns masquerade as bottles of ouzo. The Parthenon becomes a basket for nuts and raisins, the Phaistós Disk a cocktail mat, key-ring or ear-ring, the Charioteer of Delphi a bedside lamp, a statue of Poseidon a garden dwarf.

Textiles

Crete is well known for its beautiful fabrics. Formerly, the wool was carded and spun by hand all over the island. Many Cretan villages still have working looms. The grade of materials runs from very fine to the coarsest goat-hair for masochistic monks. Manufactured articles range from bedspreads

Legendary Minoan and Cretan scenes are remembered in hand-painted ceramic pots.

and pillow covers, curtains, throw-rugs and wall-hangings to those brightly coloured Greek *tagária* shoulder bags – in Crete more frequently known as *voúrgia*. You can also buy the material by the bolt – most shops will ship it for you.

Sports

The athletes of ancient Crete returning to see what's happening on the island these days might be puzzled by all the swimming. In their day, swimming was something you did to escape a shipwreck. On the other hand, not many people do much bull-leaping or wrestling these days.

The coastal resorts and mountainous interior provide admirable playgrounds for all kinds of activities in addition to swimming. You'll find that the major resorts all rent out boats and other equipmen and. in even the tiniest, secluded fishing harbour you should find a caïque to hire, though the island's sudden unpredictable **89**

Flora and Fauna

Botanists have accounted for more than 1500 species of plant, of which 182 are exclusive to Crete. In winter, white sprays of almond blossom in the lowlands compete with the snow of the mountain peaks. The ground is carpeted with small white narcissus, pink and lavender anemones and wild orchids of every variety.

The winter flowers continue into spring, joined by the waxy-yellow prickly pear flowers, asphodel and iris. The *Iris Cretensis*, with an orange stripe against a blue background, is a variety peculiar to (and named after) the island. The hills cloak themselves in bright yellow gorse and broom and the fields turn into blankets of daisies, dotted with scarlet wild tulips and poppies.

Summer Sweetness

During the summer, bougainvillea flows over the walls of ancient ruins and garden walls, along with sweet-smelling jasmine and honeysuckle. White and pink oleander proliferate. Along the roadsides, the gigantic candelabra of *agave americana* must wait 10 to 15 years before it blooms, just once, and then dies. And the countryside is redolent with the flowering thyme that gives Cretan honey its distinctive flavour. Thyme and bees are inseparable here.

Hills turn mauve with heather in the autumn. Domestic flower-gardens form a patchwork of zinnias, geraniums and chrysanthemums. With the winter rains, purple and saffron crocuses and brilliant cyclamen appear. Winter is the time, too, when oranges and lemons ripen to add their colour to the landscape.

Among the profusion of Crete's **herbs**, the one that has been associated with the island since antiquity is dittany or *origanum dictamnus*, or *díktamo*, as the Cretans call it. Named after Mount Díkti, it was regarded as an ideal antidote to arrow-wounds and is now served as a herbal tea to soothe whatever else ails you.

Oil and Beans

In Minoan times, cypress trees covered the island. Deforestation and neglect have reduced their number to a tiny few, clustered mainly along the west coast. The one tree that grows everywhere is the gnarled **olive**, whole groves of them glistening silver when their leaves are turned by the wind, their oil providing a major source of export revenue. Another important tree is the carob, especially dense in the eastern half of the island. It is known also as 'St. John's bread' because John the Baptist was supposed to have lived off its beans while wandering in the wilderness. The red-podded carob beans, fodder for man and beast, were the source of the jeweller's term *carat*, from the Greek *keration* ('little horn'), referring to the tough, horny little carob bean once used as the standard of measure.

Goats and Owls

Besides the ever-present and practical donkey, the island's most important animal is the Cretan ibex or *agrími*, also called the *kri-kri*. A large but nimble goat with sweeping horns, the *agrími* was frequently depicted in Minoan art. Today it is found in its wild state only in the heights above the Samariá Gorge and, as a protected herd, on a tiny island-reserve in Mirabéllo Bay.

In the mountains, you may spot griffon vultures, falcons and eagles as well as the hoopoe, bee-eater and owls. The island also receives annual visits from noisy flocks of migratory swallows.

91

*S*oaring high above the waves attached to a paraglider is one way to get good views.

winds make sailing somewhat hazardous and frustrating.

Swimming

The seas around the island are warm enough for swimming from May to mid-October. **92** With scores of beaches to choose from, picking the right one is not always obvious. The ideal beach is not always the one with the finest sand. Pebble beaches are preferable for the days when the *méltemi* wind is blowing. Rock-ledge beaches have the considerable advantage of being uncrowded, but you should wear plastic sandals to paddle around on the rocks.

For children, make sure you have some really safe shallow bathing available as lifeguards are rare to non-existent. Nudist bathing is officially forbidden, but in practice, you will find several beaches where people take it all off, the criterion for which seems to be relatively secluded places not frequented by families or by the Greeks themselves. Take care not to offend.

As for pollution, the obvious beaches to avoid are those close to Iráklion. The European Commission's Blue Flag for top-rated cleanliness has recently been awarded to Vaï and Eloúnda and the Green Flag for clean waters went to Chersonísos. There may be more potential award winners from 24,000 km (15,000 miles) of coastline.

Snorkelling and Scuba Diving

The joy of underwater swimming is not just for the marine life you will see, but also the vestiges of ancient ports and cities. On Mirabéllo Bay, you can swim out from Eloúnda Beach to see the submerged ruins of Oloús, a Greco-Roman settlement. Across the bay, part of the Minoan ruins of Móchlos are also underwater. But for the most part, you will have to content yourself with glimpses snatched from snorkelling. Like underwater photography, scuba diving is restricted to government designated areas where you cannot disturb ancient shipwrecks or archaeological sites.

Windsurfing and Waterskiing

Ágios Nikólaos, Eloúnda, Sitía and Ierápetra all provide rental equipment. Adepts of both sports appreciate the shelter of Mirabéllo Bay, but they are asked increasingly to steer clear of popular family beaches. Waterskiing is very popular at Knossós Beach, and resorts immediately around Réthimnon have first-class facilities for paragliding and jet-skiing.

Fishing

Shore fishing or from a boat can catch you seabass, swordfish, dentex and a host of Mediterranean fish. No special licence is needed, but underwater spear fishing is restricted. It is sometimes possible to 'hitch a ride' with a friendly fishermen going out at night to fish with flare lanterns. Another, even more useful friend is the local taverna chef who may cook your catch.

Tennis

Most big resort hotels have hard courts, Chaniá and Iráklion both have tennis clubs, and there are public courts in Iráklion behind the Archaeological Museum.

93

*F*ishing has long been a way of life on Crete. Rent a boat or hitch a ride with a local.

Hiking and Climbing

Iráklion, Réthimnon and Chaniá have clubs which organize hiking excursions into the mountains. Foreigners are welcome to join and the local tourist office will give you details. More ambitious climbers aiming at Mount Ida or peaks in the Levka Mountains should enquire at the Greek Alpine Club in Chaniá for information about guides and equipment.

Entertainment

Hotels make an effort to put on evenings of 'authentic traditional' entertainment to give guests a taste of island culture

The Vólta

The entertainment the Cretans themselves most enjoy is their own conversation. The *vólta* (evening stroll, a veritable parade) along the harbour promenade or around the main town square and then an hour or two at a café under the plane trees, is their daily theatre. The curtain rises with a fulsome greeting or – drama – a cold snub. Who is wooing whom? *That's* her new fiancé? Will his rich uncle from America buy the supermarket? What about the building promoter's 'heart attack'? The pleasure is contagious and infects the hitherto most introverted visitor from less demonstrative climes. To execute an authentic *vólta*, you should dress with a certain decorum, let's say casual elegance. No camera, no baseball cap, no shopping bag. Arm in arm rather than hand in hand, and you're set to join the gossiping throng.

95

which is fast fading in the resort towns, but can still be found in remoter inland communities. These have everything you could wish for – music, dancing, costumes – except the company of the Cretans themselves with which to enjoy them. To find the real thing, you must explore the mountain villages.

Music and Dance

Greek **music** is more than the ubiquitous twang from movie themes like *Zorba the Greek*, but the power of modern sound-

---

FESTIVALS

Despite the island's rapid modernization, the Cretans are still strongly attached to their old traditions, cultural, religious and pagan.

January 1: New Year's Day or *Protochroniá* – St Basil's Day, in whose name you may be offered a sprig of basil, symbol of hospitality. For good luck, gamblers see the New Year in around the card table.

January 6: for Epiphany (*ton Theofaníon*), a cross is thrown into the harbour, and young men dive into the icy waters to retrieve it. The one who recovers it receives a special blessing and a crucifix.

February: the two weeks before Lent (*Apókries*) are boisterously celebrated with a carnival in Iráklion and Réthimnon.

Clean Monday: (*Katharí Deftéra*) first day of Orthodox Lent, general house cleaning, laundry and kite-flying; frugal meals of *lagána* (unleavened bread) and *taramá* (salty fish eggs), olives without oil, and *halvá* (sesame paste cake).

Orthodox Easter: candlelit funeral processions follow a flower-bedecked sculpted bier on Good Friday (*Megáli Paraskeví*). On Holy Saturday, Judas is burned in effigy, fire-

amplifying systems is increasing all the time. Some purists claim that the long-necked mandolin-like *bouzoúki* instrument, which has given its name to the music and the nightclubs in which it is performed, is not even Greek, but Turkish.

The *syrtáki* **dance** popularized by Anthony Quinn's Zorba is in fact a combination, invented for the film, of several distinct traditional dances. The *zeybékiko*, coming originally from Asia Minor, is an introspective dance of meditation with the man swaying slowly,

---

works are let off, and at midnight, the priest hands down the sacred flame from candle to candle for each household to light an oil lamp. On Sunday (*Páscha*), thousands of lambs are sacrificed for roasting, exactly as in ancient Greece at the approach of spring.

May 21: the Allies' courageous 1941 Battle of Crete is commemorated at Chaniá with three days of music and dancing.

May 25: Chóra Sfakíon celebrates Greek Independence.

June 24: bonfires are lit for John the Baptist (*tou Agíou Ioánnou*), with boys jumping over the embers.

July: Wine Festival in Réthimnon including wine sampling, music and dancing.

July/August: Renaissanace and Music Festivals in Réthimnon.

August 15: for Assumption Day (*tis Panangías*), there are fireworks, a craftwork fair and dancing at Móchlos (near Mália); processions at Neápolis (near Ágios Nikólaos) and Chrisoskalítissa Convent.

November 7-9: Crete's 'national holiday' celebrates the 1866 explosion at the Monastery of Arkádi (see p.xx). Festivities both at the monastery and in Réthimnon.

November 11: Iráklion commemorates its patron saint, Minas.

arms outstretched, eyes half closed, leaning backwards, bending his knees, occasionally taking long steps sideways or forwards like a drugged flamingo and making a sudden sharp twist or leap before retrieving his more deliberate rhythm. This blossoms into the *khassápikos* or butcher's dance in which two or three men join arms and find a community of spirit by swaying, dipping and stepping together, the sudden changes signalled by a shout or squeeze of the shoulder from the lead dancer carrying a handkerchief. These dances are in turn linked to the slow, majestic *tsamíko* performed originally by the *kléphtes* mountain rebels, a dragging-round dance known as the *syrtós,* and Crete's very own hop-dance, the *soústa.* The dances' ancient origins can be seen in the formations of dancers in the Minoan friezes at Knossós (see p.36).

The hybrid *syrtáki* is performed at hosts of resort tavernas and nightclubs. Here, the dancers may smash plates or toss gardenias, according to their temperament (both are added to the bill). You can, of course, join in. The best chance of seeing the more traditional dances is at country weddings and festivals.

Symphonic and choral **music** are performed at Réthimnon's summer arts festivals. Tickets can be hard to come by unless you book well in advance, but the bigger hotels can sometimes help, at slightly higher prices.

Cinema

In the summer, **films** are always shown in the open air. Cinephiles must bow to the custom of a sudden 20-minute break in the middle for refreshment. The Greeks do not dub their foreign films, everything is presented in its original version with Greek subtitles. This may have the strange effect of the Greeks in the audience laughing before you do, as the subtitles translate the jokes faster than they are spoken. But you can get your own back, since not all the jokes are seemingly always translated.

Eating Out

The basic ingredients of a Greek meal have not really changed since Plato's Banquet. At an Easter dinner in a Cretan mountain village, lamb, goat and veal are charcoal grilled much as they were by Agamemnon's soldiers at the gates of Troy. The olives, oil and lemon, basil and oregano, figs and almonds, even the resinous taste of the wine all form a gastronomic link between Greece ancient and modern.

Ambiance is more important at the Cretan dinner table than *haute cuisine*. Greek cooking makes no pretence of emulating the sophistication of the French or the infinite variety of the Chinese. Yet the people's natural zest for life can always conjure the savoury ingredients of a Mediterranean market into something wholesome, satisfying and not without its own subtlety.

Greek or Turkish

Nothing makes the Greeks more angry – particularly Cretans – than to hear they have no cuisine of their own. Detractors dismiss it as a mishmash of their numerous conquerors, the last to date being the Turks, establishing, for example, a proprietary claim to the thick coffee and honey-drenched pastries. But even these, the Greeks insist, are Greek in origin.

Classical Greek cooking had much in common with French *nouvelle cuisine*: finesse in simplicity and authentic tastes using just herbs and a very few basic ingredients. In Plato's *Republic*, frugal Socrates proposes an ideal diet that would serve very well for your mid-day holiday meal: bread, olives, cheese, vegetables and fruit. Epicurus, who held that the highest good is pleasure but not necessarily self-indulgence, declared: 'simple dishes are as satisfying as sumptuous banquets.'

WHERE TO GO

You will never discover the adventure of Greek cooking if you stick to your hotel dining room. Pandering to palates intimidated by 'strange' dishes, hotel cooking remains unadventurous. Even when a local 'speciality' is offered, like the yoghurt and cucumber appetizer known as *dzadzíki*, the garlic essential to its taste is almost imperceptible, on the assumption that it might be upsetting.

Try, whenever possible, to go where the Cretans go. In the coastal resorts, for instance, the islanders often keep away from the crowded harbourside establishments. In the back-street taverna, you can enjoy the real zing of a garlicky *dzadzíki*, often rendered more refreshing with an added touch of mint.

One of the greatest pleasures on Crete is the gastronomic possibilities. Good food sampled al fresco is a very pleasant experience.

Look out for three varieties of snack bar. For yoghurt or cheese snacks, try the *galaktopolío* (dairy counter). The *psistariá* (grill) serves different kinds of meat kebab. For a better selection of desserts than you'll find in restaurants, go to the *zacharoplastío* (pastry shop).

You will also come across the traditional Greek *kafenion* (café), particularly in the mountain villages. But this is more of a men's club than a public café, popular for political debate, backgammon and very strong coffee. Strangers are not unwelcome, but the place is considered, if not off limits, then at least a haven for Greeks among themselves where outsiders should remain discreet – understandable on such a tourist-saturated island.

WHEN TO GO

If you decide to 'go native' and accept wholeheartedly the institution of the afternoon siesta, you may want to modify your meal times. The Cretans themselves put in a prolonged morning's work and have lunch around 2 p.m., siesta until 5 p.m., maybe work some more until 8.30 p.m. and then dine late at around 9.30 p.m. Restaurants will serve you earlier, from midday and early evening, but you'll miss the authentic Cretan scene if you keep to 'tourist hours'.

THE MENU

The tantalizing thing about the tasty Greek specialities we will describe here is that only a fraction of them are available at any one time. The menu in English often contains them all, but only those items with a price against them are being served that day. Rather than submit to this frustration, do what the Greeks do and go into the kitchen to see what is being cooked. The management will be more than happy for you to point out your choices here and avoid later misunderstandings. Remember fish and meat are often priced by weight, so that the size you choose in the kitchen becomes your responsibility when the bill arrives. **101**

Appetizers

It is the Greek custom to eat appetizers (*mezédes*), accompanied by an aperitif of ouzo and water, separately from the main meal. For convenience, they are usually served at resort tavernas as part of the dinner. But the essence of the *meze* is its leisurely enjoyment, something to savour for itself. You could make a whole meal just from the *mezédes*, but go easy on the quantities – some of the dishes are quite rich for the unaccustomed stomach.

The range is impressive: *taramá* (a creamy paste of cod's roe mixed with breadcrumbs, egg yolk, lemon juice, salt, pepper and olive oil), *dolmádes* (little parcels of vine leaves, filled with rice and pine kernels, braised in olive oil and lemon and served cold), *melitzanosaláta* (aubergine salad pureed with onion and garlic), *saláta choriátiki* (the ubiquitous Greek salad – literally 'village salad' – a refreshing mixture of tomato, cucumber, feta cheese and black olives), *kalamarákia tiganitá* (small pieces of fried squid), *tirópitakia* (small pastry triangles of goat and ewe cheese), *salingária* (Cretan snails), and, of course, dishes of olives, green, black, brown or silvery.

Soups

The most famous, *avgolémono* (egg and lemon with chicken broth, thickened with rice), is light enough to appear as an accompaniment. Cretan soups of *fasólia* (bean), *fakés* (lentil), or *revíthia* (chickpea) are excellent. Good seafood restaurants keep a cauldron of *psarósoupa* (fish soup) going or occasionally *kalamariáki* (a spicy squid and tomato soup).

Fish

The surest pleasure of the Greek table is its seafood. Go down to the harbour to see what has been caught that day. For your personal choice of fish, the trip back to the kitchen becomes really important. Simplest is often best: have the fish grilled – *barboúnia* (red mullet), *xifías* (swordfish), often served on the skewer, *glóssa* (sole), and *lithríni* (bream) are among the most popular. *Sardéles* (sardines) are good baked and *marídes* (whitebait) are served fried. You may come across a host of other Greek fish which have no unanimously accepted English equivalents. The 'lobster' proposed on some menus is almost invariably a clawless crustacean properly known as crayfish or rock lobster. If you like your seafood stewed, try octopus with white wine, tomatoes and potatoes, or *garídes* (prawns) in white wine and feta cheese.

Meat

Your first encounter with meat specialities is likely to be at the *psistariá* snack bar serving *souvlákia* (garlic-marinated lamb kebabs with onions), and *gíros* (slices of meat from spit-roasted cones of pork, veal or lamb – also known as *donér kebáb*). This latter often comes with bread and salad. Tavernas may serve *souvlákia*, along with *keftédes* (spicy lamb meat balls). In country villages, you can find superb *katzíka* (goat meat dishes served in a tomato sauce or even stewed in *avgolémono* soup). Crete is celebrated for its *stiffádo* (braised beef with onions). *Brizoles* (grilled steak) will generally come well done unless you specify otherwise, and is not usually tender enough to risk less than medium. *Moussaká* has many variations, but basically alternates layers of sliced aubergine with chopped lamb, onions and béchamel sauce topped with a layer of aubergine skins.

Cheese

Cheeses are generally made out of sheep's or goat's milk. *Feta* is the best known of the soft cheeses, popping up in almost every delicious Greek salad. Crete's *anthótyro* and *manoúri* are relatively bland, *graviéera* is harder and sharper. Other hard cheeses are the *agrafáou* and the salty *kefalotíri*. A rare blue cheese to hold its own against any French variety is *kopanistí*.

Dessert

The Greeks eat their after-dinner dessert at the *zacharoplastío* (pastry shop) on the way home. Tavernas rarely have a full selection.

Among the most popular (all, you will notice, containing plenty of honey) are: *baklavá* (a honey-drenched flaky pastry with walnuts and almonds), *loukoúm* (a doughnut-like honey fritter), *kataífi* (a sort of shredded wheat filled with honey or syrup and chopped almonds), *pítta me méli* (honey cake). Clearly of Venetian inspiration, *rizógalo* is a creamy-smooth rice pudding. *Galak- toboúriko* is a refreshing custard pie.

And remember at the dairy shop (*galaktopolío*) you can pick up the perfect sour-sweet mixture of fresh yoghurt and honey. The best of the fruit are the pomegranates, peaches, apricots, grapes and melon.

*C*rete is an island of infinite variety, not least in its breads. Fruit is first-class.

Bread

One of the sweetest-smelling places in a Cretan village is the bakery. If you are shopping for a picnic, get here early for the freshest *kouloúria* rings of white bread sprinkled with sesame seeds. *Choriátiko* is country bread, flat, off-white and very tasty. And take along a few *moustalevriá* (wine-flavoured sesame biscuits). At the end of the day, the ovens

are made available for neighbours' family roasts. If you have rented a house, make friends with the baker and he will do your leg of lamb too.

DRINKS
Coffee

Unless you prefer bland instant (known imaginatively here as *nes*), make the little effort to get the thick black Levantine brew that they do *not* call Turkish coffee. *Ellinikó* is what you say for the traditional coffee served, grounds and all, from a long-handled copper or aluminium pot. But to be sure of getting it freshly brewed to your liking, correctly served with an accompanying glass of iced water, add *éna vari glikó* (heavy and sweet), *glykí vastró* (sweet but boiled thinner), *éna métrio* (medium), or *éna skéto* (without sugar).

Wine and Beer

Greek wine had a much better reputation in the ancient world than it does now, though Cretan wines are still considered a notch above the rest you might find in Greece or on any of its islands.

Retsina, the unique resinous white wine, was a favourite of the ancient Greeks. Today, pine resin is still added in fermentation to permit longer conservation in a hot climate. It takes a short time to acquire the taste and discover how well it goes with both seafood and lamb. The Cretan variety seems to be less acid than that from the mainland.

Although selections from most Greek wineries are available, try the local white wine (*áspro*) of Olympia, Minos, Logado, Górtis and Lató. Go easier on the red (*mávro* – 'black'), notoriously full-bodied and rich in alcohol. The best local reds come from Sitía. House wines served in a carafe tend to be dark rosé (*kókkino*). **105**

Local beer is mostly locally brewed under licence from good German parent companies.

If you develop a taste for aniseed-flavoured *oúzo*, served with the *mezédes* neat or with ice and water, one of the finest is Plomari imported from Lesbos. Cretans often prefer a shot (or two) of *rakí*, sometimes called *tsikoudiá* – stronger than *oúzo* but closer in flavour to the French *marc* or Italian *grappa*. Strongest of all is Réthimnon's *mournorakí*, made from mulberries. For those who like something sweeter, Crete's tangerines make a pleasant liqueur called *mandaríni*.

To Help You Order

could we have a table?		**tha boroúsame na échoume éna trapézi?**		
I'd like a/ an/some...	**tha íthela...**	mineral water	**metallikó neró**	
beer	**mía bíra**	napkin	**éna trapezo**	
bread	**psomí**		**mándilo**	
coffee	**éna kafé**	potatoes	**patátes**	
cutlery	**macheropírouna**	rice	**rízi**	
dessert	**éna glíko**	salad	**mía saláta**	
fish	**psári**	soup	**mía soúpa**	
fruit	**froúta**	sugar	**záchari**	
glass	**éna potíri**	tea	**éna tsaï**	
ice-cream	**éna pagotó**	(iced)		
meat	**kréas**	water	**(pagoméno) neró**	
milk	**gála**	wine	**krasí**	

BLUEPRINT
for a
Perfect Trip

An A–Z Summary of Practical Information and Facts

Listed after most main entries is an appropriate Greek transla-
tion, usually in the singular. You will find this vocabulary useful when asking for information or assistance.

A star (*) following an entry indicates that relevant prices are
to be found under PLANNING YOUR BUDGET (see p.127).

A

ACCOMMODATION* (ΔΩΜΑΤΙΑ – domátia)

Accommodation on Crete ranges from the rustic comfort of a small
room in a country village to the luxury of a hotel-bungalow complex
in a beach resort.

Hotels (ΞΕΝΟΔΟΧΕΙΟ – xenodochío) At the Greek National
Tourist Office, locally signposted 'EOT' (Ellinikós Organismós
Tourismoú), and most good travel agents, you can consult a comprehensive index of hotels listed by price and category. To help you
with the enormous number of choices, we shortlist a few of them in
the RECOMMENDED HOTELS section – see p.66.

In high season, the large hotels are almost invariably booked up
long in advance by package-tour organizations, but no matter where
you are or what time of the day or night it may be, a room will
usually be found for you somewhere. One solution, quite delightful
on a warm, starry night, is 'roof-space' – whereby cheaper hotels or
tavernas offer a mattress on their roof.

The hotels are divided into 6 classes: Luxury, A, B, C, D and E.
Prices are government controlled. Some extras may (legitimately) be
added, such as air conditioning or television, but the rate for the
room must be displayed somewhere in the room. Reductions can
usually be arranged for children. To avoid unpleasant surprises with
your bill, check in advance. During high season, for instance, hotel

management may insist on your taking at least half board. The advantage of hotels without restaurants (Class C and down) is that you will not be pinned down by half-board obligations and can explore more outside restaurants.

Private Accommodation. Staying in the Cretans' own homes is often the best way to get to know the islanders, but increasingly, especially in the main resorts, rooms are purpose-built in character-less modern blocks. However, in country villages away from the coast you can find pleasant rooms, with bath or shower and often with cooking facilities. The now accepted sign to look for (in English) is 'Rent Room' – if the sign is neon, don't expect anything characterful.

Villas. These range from small, simple cottages to quite lavish summer houses, let on a monthly or even weekly basis. When booking, ascertain the complete facilities – which normally (but not always), include refrigerator, hot water and electricity. (See also CAMPING and YOUTH HOSTELS.)

I'd like a single/double room	**Tha íthela éna monó/dipló domátio**
with bath/shower.	**me bánion/dous.**
What's the rate per night?	**Piá íne i timí giá mía níkta?**

AIRPORTS (*aerodrómio*)

Crete has three airports. Almost all international flights come into Iráklion. The other two, near Chaniá and Sitía, are served by Olympic Airways and smaller charter companies via Athens.

Iráklion airport offers a wide range of car-hire firms and travel agency counters as well as the usual amenities of restaurant, snack-bar and duty-free shop. Taxis are plentiful in addition to public and airport bus services to take you into town.

Porter!	**Achthofóre!**
Taxi!	**Taxí!**
Where's the bus for...?	**Pou íne to leoforío giá...?**

ALPHABET

(See also LANGUAGE and p.106.) The exotic letters of the Greek alphabet need not be a mystery to you. Below we have listed the Greek letters in their capital and small forms, followed by the letters they correspond to in English.

Stress, a very important feature of the Greek language, is indicated throughout this guide by an accent mark (´) above the vowel of the symbol to be stressed. Accentuate the wrong syllable and you may evoke puzzlement or total misunderstanding in your listener.

A	α	a	as in bar
B	β	v	
Γ	γ	g	as in go*
Δ	δ	d	like **th** in **this**
E	ε	e	as in get
Z	ζ	z	
H	η	i	like **ee** in meet
Θ	θ	th	as in **thin**
I	ι	i	like **ee** in meet
K	κ	k	
Λ	λ	l	
M	μ	m	
N	ν	n	
Ξ	ξ	x	like **ks** in thanks
O	o	o	as in bone
Π	π	p	
P	ρ	r	
Σ	σ,ς	s	as in kiss
T	τ	t	
Y	υ	i	like **ee** in meet
Φ	φ	f	
X	χ	ch	as in Scottish lo**ch**
Ψ	ψ	ps	as in ti**psy**
Ω	ω	o	as in bone
OY	ου	ou	as in soup

110 * except before **i**- and **e**-sounds, when it's pronounced like **y** in yes

ANTIQUITIES (*archéa*)

Since the exploits of 19th-century robbers of tombs and temples, antiquities may be exported only with the approval of the Archaeological Council and the Greek Ministry of Culture and Science. Law-breakers face a stiff fine and a prison sentence of up to five years. Beachcombers should not even *think* of using a metal-detector – totally illegal. If you do stumble upon an ancient amphora or are offered a 'genuine Byzantine icon', contact the head of the local museum, *before* handing over any money, to find out if you may take it home with you and if so, the correct procedure to follow.

B

BICYCLE AND MOTORBIKE HIRE* (*enikiásis podiláton/motopodiláton*)

This is a thriving business in all the resort towns. In high season, you should stake your claim early on Sundays and public holidays when the Greeks join the throng. Make sure the price includes proper insurance. Motor scooters are best used in town and on flat coastal roads – the interior is too hilly for anything but a motorbike. Remember that it is illegal to ride motorbikes during siesta hours (2 p.m. to 6 p.m.) and after 11 p.m.

C

CAMPING* (ΚΑΜΠΙΝΓΚ – '*camping*')

Only official campsites may be used. There are a dozen of them open from May to September – a complete list with telephone numbers is available from the Greek National Tourist Office. The most popular on the north coast are near Iráklion, Chersonísos and Mália and on the south coast at Ierápetra, Mátala, Agía Galíni and Paleochóra.

May we camp here?   **Boroúme na kataskinósoume edó?**

We have a tent	**Échoume mía skiní**
Can I hire/buy a sleeping bag?	**Boró na nikiáso/agoráso éna 'sleeping bag'?**

CAR HIRE* (ΕΝΟΙΚΙΑΣΕΙΣ ΑΦΤΟΚΙΝΗΤΩΝ – *enikiásis aftokiníton*)

Local companies offer increasingly competitive prices compared with the fixed rates of the major international rental firms, especially off season. However, if you're booking in advance from home, the big firms are the best bet in high season if you want to be sure of a car, as the number of vehicles available from local companies may be limited at your resort.

Locally, it is wiser to rent your car with a credit card than have to haggle over the amount of reimbursement from a cash deposit. Make sure of the exact nature of the insurance, third-party or complete coverage, included in or added to the quoted price.

Although the law requires an International Driving Permit for all foreigners renting a car in Greece, in practice agencies accept any valid national licence that has been held for at least one year.

I'd like to rent a car tomorrow.	**Tha íthela na nikiáso éna aftokínito ávrio.**
for one day/a week	**giá mía iméra/mía evdomáda**

CLIMATE

Crete has a good climate throughout the year and is becoming increasingly popular as a winter destination for tourists fleeing the cold (and the crowds). Even in the coolest months of January and February, the temperature seldom drops below 8°C (46°F). The hardy go skiing in the Levka Mountains and get their suntan down on the beach. Spring is short, but beautifully green and usually with some rain in April; summers are baking hot and autumn brings more rain, in October.

Approximate monthly average temperatures (Iráklion):

		J	F	M	A	M	J	J	A	S	O	N	D
Air	Max. °C	16	16	18	21	24	28	30	30	28	26	21	19
	°F	60	60	64	70	76	82	86	86	82	78	70	66
	Min. °C	9	9	10	12	16	18	20	22	20	17	14	11
	°F	48	48	50	54	60	64	68	72	68	62	57	52
Sea temp.	°C	16	16	17	18	20	23	24	25	24	23	19	17
	°F	61	61	63	64	68	73	75	77	75	73	66	63

CLOTHING (*rouchismós*)

There's nothing formal about everyday life on Crete. A tie is practically never expected, even in the smartest restaurant, and a jacket only rarely. However, many hotel dining-rooms discourage shorts in the evening. Similarly, put on a shirt or sarong for the trip to or from the beach.

One place where decorum really does matter is in a church or monastery. Women are expected to dress modestly, and no-one should wear shorts.

Bring a sweater even for summer evenings, especially for trips up into the mountains, and light rainwear for visits in the spring or autumn. In the summer, some kind of hat and sunglasses are recommended. Good sandals or 'thongs' can be bought on the island to protect against the hot sand or rocks. One absolute must: sturdy, comfortable shoes for visits to historical sites like Knossós or rambles in the mountains.

Will I need a jacket and tie?	**Tha chriastó sakáki ke graváta?**
Is it all right if I wear this?	**Tha íme endáxi an foréso aftó?**

113

COMPLAINTS (*parápona*)

If you really feel you have been cheated or misled, raise the matter first with the manager or proprietor of the establishment in question. If you still do not get satisfaction, take the problem to the Tourist Police, telephone 171 (see POLICE). Often, just mentioning the words 'Tourist Police' should get results, and complaints with a smile are much more effective than angry glares or shouting.

CONSULATES AND EMBASSIES (*proxenío; presvía*)

While the embassies are of course all in Athens, some countries have consulates in Iráklion. Contact the consulate or embassy of your home country only if things go *seriously* wrong – for a lost passport, trouble with the police, or an accident. The consulate can issue emergency passports, give advice on obtaining money from home, and provide a list of lawyers, doctors and interpreters for emergency situations. It cannot pay your bills, lend you money, find you a job or obtain a work permit for you. Hours vary, so call before going to the following addresses:

British Consulate (also for citizens of Eire and Commonwealth countries not separately represented):

Papalexándrou St 16, Iráklion; tel. (081) 224 012.

Canadian Embassy:

Gennadiou 4, Ypsilántou, 115-121 Athens; tel. (01) 723 9511.

U.S. Embassy:

Leofóros Vass. Sofías 91, 101-160 Athens; tel. (01) 721 2951.

CRIME (*églima*)

Crime is relatively rare on Crete. If you leave something in a shop or restaurant, the proprietor will do his best to find it. Honesty is a matter of pride among Cretans. Your biggest risk is more likely to come from your fellow tourists, so take the precaution of locking up your valuables, and watch your handbag in public.

114 I want to report a theft.   **Thélo na katangílo mía klopí.**

CUSTOMS AND ENTRY FORMALITIES

Visitors from EC countries only need an identity card to enter Greece. Citizens of most other countries must have a valid passport. Though European and North American residents are not subject to any health requirements, visitors from further afield may require a smallpox vaccination. Check with a travel agent before departure.

The following chart shows the quantities of certain major items you may take into Greece and, upon returning home, into your own country:

Into:	Cigarettes		Cigars		Tobacco	Spirits		Wine
Greece 1)	300	or	75	or	400g	1.5L	and	5L
2)	200	or	50	or	250g	1L	and	2L
3)	400	or	100	or	500g	1L	and	2L
Canada	200	and	50	and	900g	1.1L	or	1L
Eire	200	or	50	or	250g	1L	and	2L
UK	200	or	50	or	250g	1L	and	2L
USA	200	and	100	and	4)	1L	or	1L

1) Visitors arriving from EEC countries with duty paid on items.
2) Visitors arriving from EEC countries with duty-free items, or from other European countries.
3) Residents outside Europe.
4) A reasonable quality.

Certain prescription drugs, including tranquillizers and headache preparations, cannot be carried into the country without an official medical document. In these drug-sensitive times, fines – even jail sentences – have been imposed on the unwary tourist. **115**

CURRENCY RESTRICTIONS

Foreign visitors to Greece can bring in up to 100,000 drachmas and leave with no more than 20,000 drachmas. There is no limit to the foreign currency or traveller's cheques you may import or export, though amounts in excess of US$1000 should be declared.

I've nothing to declare.   **Den écho na dilóso típota.**

D

DISABLED TRAVELLERS

It must be said that Crete has not yet properly geared up its tourist facilities for assisting the disabled. Some hotels are adapting their amenities, but it is a slow process and you should inquire ahead of time about what precisely is available. The mountainous terrain of the interior is a major obstacle for getting around.

DRIVING

Entering Greece. Those rare travellers bringing their own vehicle onto the island need car registration papers, nationality plate or sticker, International Driving Permit (not required for British motorists) and insurance coverage (the Green Card is no longer compulsory within the EC although comprehensive coverage is advisable).

Despite the laxness you may observe on the island, it is obligatory to use seat belts, and motorbike and motorscooter drivers – as well as passengers – must wear crash helmets. The police can suddenly clamp down and fines for non-compliance are high.

Driving Conditions. The main road which extends along the north coast, connecting all the major towns, is for almost its entire length broad and well-maintained. Even during the high tourist season, traffic jams are a rarity. At the eastern end beyond Ágios Nikólaos, the scenery and hairpin bends make equally spectacular demands on your attention.

Off national highways, secondary roads are usually in good condition. On country road or national highway, sheep appear to consider themselves as sacred as cows in India. Humour them. On village streets, you should also look out for local pedestrians who are in no hurry to get out of the way, but do not expect Cretan drivers to return the compliment when *you* are the pedestrian! And never mind the local drivers' habit of passing on the right or left without warning – the non-suicidal rule remains: drive on the right, pass on the left.

Traffic Police. Patrol cars have the word POLICE in large letters on the doors. They are particularly severe on speeding and illegal parking and may give you a cash fine which you must pay on the spot.

Fuel. Service stations are plentiful on the island, but check your fuel gauge before heading for the more remote areas in the south. Unleaded fuel is now available in all the main resorts.

Fluid measures

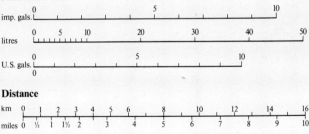

Distance

Road signs Most road signs are the standard pictographs used throughout Europe. However, you may encounter the following written signs:

ΑΔΙΕΞΟΔΟΣ	No through road
ΑΛΤ	Stop
ΑΝΩΜΑΛΙΑ ΟΔΟΣΤΡΩΜΑΤΟΣ	Bad road surface
ΑΠΑΓΟΡΕΥΕΤΑΙ Η ΑΝΑΜΟΝΗ	No waiting

ΑΠΑΓΟΡΕΥΕΤΑΙ Η ΕΙΣΟΔΟΣ	No entry
ΑΠΑΓΟΡΕΥΕΤΑΙ Η ΣΤΑΘΜΕΥΣΙΣ	No parking
ΔΙΑΒΑΣΙΣ ΠΕΖΩΝ	Pedestrian crossing
ΕΛΑΤΤΩΣΑΤΕ ΤΑΧΥΤΗΤΑΝ	Reduce speed
ΕΠΙΚΙΝΔΥΝΟΣ ΚΑΤΩΦΕΡΕΙΑ	Dangerous incline
ΕΡΓΑ ΕΠΙ ΤΗΣ ΟΔΟΥ	Roadworks in progress
ΚΙΝΔΥΝΟΣ	Caution
ΜΟΝΟΔΡΟΜΟΣ	One-way traffic
ΠΑΡΑΚΑΜΠΤΗΡΙΟΣ	Diversion (Detour)
ΠΟΔΗΛΑΤΑΙ	Cyclists
ΠΟΡΕΙΑ ΥΠΟΧΡΕΩΤΙΚΗ ΔΕΞΙΑ	Keep to the right
ΣΤΑΣΙΣ ΛΕΩΦΡΕΙΟΥ	Bus stop

(International) Driving Licence	**(diethnís) ádia odigíseos**
car registration papers	**ádia kykloforías**
Green Card	**asfália aftokinítou**
Are we on the right road for...?	**Ímaste sto sostó drómo giá...?**
Fill her up, please, top grade.	**Na to gemísete me venzíni soúper, parakaló.**
Check the oil/tires/battery.	**Na elénxete ta ládia/ta lásticha/ti bataría.**
I've broken down.	**Épatha mía vlávi.**
There's been an accident.	**Égine éna dystíchima.**

E

ELECTRIC CURRENT (*ilektrikó révma*)

You will find only 220-volt, 50-cycle A.C. on Crete. If you need a plug adaptor, check with your hotel receptionist.

an adaptor	**énas metaschimatistís**
a battery	**mía bataría**

EMERGENCIES

(See also CONSULATES on p.114 and POLICE on p.128.) Except in remoter areas, you will usually find someone who speaks English who will be able to help you. If you are alone and near a phone, here are some important numbers:

Police/Emergencies	100
Tourist Police	171
Fire	199
Road assistance	104

And here are a few words we hope you will never need to use:

Careful!	**Prosochí!**
Fire!	**Fotiá!**
Help!	**Voíthia!**
Stop thief!	**Stamatíste to kléfti!**

ETIQUETTE

Weathering the assaults of mass tourism, Greek hospitality remains by and large astonishingly sincere and generous. On Crete, its lavishness can become overwhelming. Even if you have been brought up to believe it is polite to start by saying 'No, thank you', you may hurt the feelings of your would-be host here. If you are taken aback, let your surprise be clearly appreciative, quickly subsiding into unabashed gratitude.

From the humblest ceramics shop to the most elegant jewellers, you may be offered a cup of coffee. Accepting this friendly gesture does not carry with it an obligation to buy. In a Cretan home, particularly in a country village, you will be plied with food and drink – don't feel ill at ease if you alone are served while your hostess looks on; it is a frequent traditional expression of hospitality.

Staring is not considered rude in Greece. On the contrary, it is a flattering sign of interest in you, satisfying a characteristic curiosity, and means no harm at all. In the same spirit, it is usual to ask personal questions about your family, your home, your work.

On your part, try not to wave your hand with the palm facing outwards when saying good-bye, nor to count on your fingers with the palm *up*. Known to the Greeks as *moúntsa*, this gesture is traditionally regarded as an insult – perhaps less so in the resorts where the **119**

Greeks have learned that the foreigners mean no offence by it, but still a taboo in remoter villages.

Like the Spanish *mañana*, the Greek *ávrio* means something more vague than tomorrow – at best, 'soon'. Learn to take your time and smile.

It cannot be asserted too often that the Greeks, like any other people, appreciate any effort to speak a few simple words of their language. You will be a great success in the taverna if you remember:

Bon appetit!	**kalí oréxi!**
Cheers!	**stin ygiá sas!**
Same to you! (in reply to 'Cheers')	**epísis!**

G

GETTING TO CRETE

Crete is accessible by road (using the car-ferry), rail, sea and air. The Greek National Tourist Office provides up-to-date maps and schedules to help you plan.

By Air

Scheduled flights. Most regularly scheduled flights for Crete stop in Athens. Olympic Airways runs daily services into Chaniá and Iráklion, each about 45 minutes' flight from Athens. There are numerous ways to get a lower price than the standard airfare, such as APEX and stand-by. Coming from North America, you may not find many bargain flights directly to Athens unless you fly from New York. It is worth getting a cheap flight to a major European city and going on to Greece from there.

Chartered flights and package tours. Charter flights can be the least expensive way to fly to Greece, but these tickets do have certain restrictions which you should check carefully before purchasing.

From the U.K. and Ireland: Prices vary enormously depending on accommodation and extras. Among the offers are 'theme' holidays such as a botanical or archaeological tour, or a 'keep fit' sports package. Tour operators can also give details on 'Wanderer' holidays for travellers planning a walking tour, using vouchers for accommodation in inexpensive lodgings.

From North America: There are straightforward flight/hotel arrangements, fly/drive deals and packages featuring Crete as part of 'Classical Greece' tours, often including a cruise.

By Road. It is a long haul for motorists, but the route does have the charm of literally following the road of Europe's civilization back to its Greek roots. The preferred itinerary from northern Europe is via Brussels, Munich, Belgrade and Thessaloníki to Piraeus for Crete-bound ferries. You can reduce time by driving through France and Italy to the port of Ancona, which has a direct ferry to Iráklion, or to one of the other Italian Adriatic ports with more frequent services via mainland Greece.

By Rail. Of the two main routes from Paris, the cheaper is via the Simplon Pass, Venice, Ljubljana, Belgrade and Thessaloníki. The other, more expensive but more interesting, goes via Bologna, Brindísi and Patras (the ferry crossing Brindísi-Patras is included in the fare). Both trips take two or three days with few stops along the way.

Young people under 26 can buy an *Inter-Rail Card* which allows one month of unlimited 2nd-class travel on all participating European railways. Senior citizens can obtain a *Rail Europ Senior* card allowing a 50% reduction. Anyone living outside Europe and North Africa can buy a *Eurailpass* before leaving home – this permits unlimited 1st-class travel on all participating European railways.

By Sea. Most travellers use the ferries from Italy to the Greek mainland. The main Adriatic port is Brindísi, with less frequent services from Bari and Venice, and a direct service to Iráklion from Ancona.

Cargo/passenger services are available from the U.S.A. to pick up ongoing ferries from Piraeus. Freighters cross the Atlantic three or four times a month with dates and ports of call subject to cargo requirements.

During peak season, there are many sailings each week and a daily car ferry from Piraeus to Iráklion (12 hours) and Chaniá (11 hours). They and Ágios Nikólaos have services to and from the Aegean islands, principally Rhodes, Santorini (Thera) and Mykonós.

GUIDES AND TOURS

The local tourist office can refer you to an officially recognized guide for visiting historic sites or to accompany you on a hike in the mountains.

We'd like an English-speaking guide.	**Tha thélame éna xenagó na milá i angliká.**
I need an English interpreter.	**Chriázome éna ánglo diermenéa.**

LANGUAGE

You are unlikely to have much of a language problem on Crete. Most people in contact with foreign tourists speak some English. Road signs are written in both Greek and Roman lettering, and many restaurant menus are printed in several languages, including English.

Still, you will certainly meet Greeks who speak only their own language. They actually have two languages – the classical *katharévousa*, until recently the language of the courts and parliaments and still used by a few conservative newspapers, and *dimotikí*, the spoken language and now also the official one. This is what you will hear on the Greek mainland today and, with slight variations in accents and a few special expressions, on Crete.

To help you communicate, the Berlitz phrase book and dictionary GREEK FOR TRAVELLERS is invaluable, covering most of the situations you will encounter. See also ALPHABET on p.110, the list of USEFUL EXPRESSIONS on the cover of this guide, and the phrases TO HELP YOU ORDER on p.106.

LAUNDRY AND DRY-CLEANING (ΠΛΥΝΤΗΡΙΟ; ΚΑΘΑΡΙΣΤΗΡΙΟ – *plyntírio; katharistírio*)

In July and August allow three or four days for a suit or dress to be dry-cleaned (just two days the rest of the year). Same-day service costs extra. The local laundry service is adequate but can be tough on delicate colours. And remember, if *ávrio* means tomorrow to you, it may be a vaguer proposition for the laundry.

When will it be ready? | **Póte tha íne étimo?**
I must have this for tomorrow morning. | **Prépi na íne étimo ávrio to proï.**

LOST PROPERTY

Given the general level of honesty among Cretans, the chances of recovering lost property are very good. If you have problems, call the tourist police (tel. 171, see POLICE).

I've lost my wallet/ handbag/passport. | **Échasa to portofóli mou/ti tsánda mou/to diavitirió mou.**

M

MEDICAL CARE

To be on the safe side, take out health insurance back home covering the risk of illness or accident while you are on holiday. Emergency treatment on Crete is free, but you will generally get better medical care if you have insurance. British citizens are entitled to the same health cover as the Greeks, but they should apply to the Department of Health and Social Security for a special form before leaving the United Kingdom.

The two main health hazards are sunburn and minor stomach upsets. Work on your tan gradually, using a strong sun-filter cream and avoiding the midday sun. Wear a hat and sunglasses. Moderation in eating and drinking should help ease you into the change of diet.

To combat mosquito attacks, buy an inflammable coil called *katól* – they hate it. If you step on a sea urchin, apply lemon juice or olive **123** oil (some suggest a well mixed dressing of both!). A jellyfish sting can be relieved by ammonia, but in case of severe swelling, see a doctor.

Pharmacies (ΦΑΡΜΑΚΕΙΟ – *farmakío*) These are easily recognizable by the sign of a red or blue cross on a white background. You will find at least one on 24-hour duty in each major town. They may not stock your personal medications and favourite remedies, so bring a reasonable supply (but see under CUSTOMS for regulations concerning prescription drugs).

Where's the nearest (all-night) pharmacy?	**Pou íne to kodinótero (dianiterévon) famarkío?**
I need a/an...	**Chiázome éna...**
doctor	**giatró**
dentist	**odontogiatrós**
ambulance	**asthenofóro**
hospital	**nosokomío**
sunstroke	**ilíasi**
fever	**piretós**
upset stomach	**varistomachiá**

MONEY MATTERS

The monetary unit of Greece is the drachma.

Coins: 1, 2, 5, 10, 20, 50 drachmas.

Banknotes: 50, 100, 500, 1,000, 5,000 drachmas.

For currency restrictions, see CUSTOMS AND ENTRY FORMALITIES.

Banks (ΤΡΑΠΕΖΑ – *trápeza*). The advantage of a better exchange rate at the banks should be weighed against the tiresomeness of a frequently long wait at their counters. The bank rate will be better than you get in restaurants or shops, but you may prefer paying your hotel's commission as a fee for the convenience. Note that the main post offices also provide currency exchange facilities. Always take your passport with you when you go to exchange money or to cash traveller's cheques. See also OPENING HOURS.

Credit Cards and Traveller's Cheques. Shops, banks, most hotels and an increasing number of resort restaurants accept the major credit cards. Traveller's cheques are best cashed at the bank or your hotel. Do *not* risk using your cashcard – too many machines still prefer to gobble it up rather than pay out money.

I want to change some pounds/dollars.	**Thélo na alláxo merikés líres/dollária.**
What's the exchange rate?	**Pía íne i timí sinallágmatos?**
Do you accept credit cards/traveller's cheques?	**Pérnete pistotikí kárta/'traveller's cheques'?**

NEWSPAPERS AND MAGAZINES (*efimerída; periodikó*)

Most foreign dailies – including the principal British newspapers and the Paris-based *International Herald Tribune* – arrive on Crete one day late. The major hotels are often the best place to find weekly newspapers and magazines.

Have you any English-language newspapers?	**Échete anglikés efimerídes?**

OPENING HOURS

Opening hours are fitted in, it sometimes seems reluctantly, around the all-important siesta. With the exception of a few tourist-geared shops, everything starts closing down at 1.30 p.m. and opens again around 4 or 5 p.m. Noise is very much frowned upon between these hours. Work resumes again after the siesta until around 9 p.m.

Banks. In general they are open 8 a.m. to 2 p.m. Monday to Friday. In summer at least one bank remains open in larger towns from 5 to 7 p.m. and for short periods on Saturdays for money changing only.

Museums and Historical Sites. Hours vary from year to year and town to town, so check with the local tourist information office. Musems and sites are always closed on national holidays.

Post Offices. In the main towns 8 a.m. to 7 p.m.; in smaller places only until 2 p.m.

Restaurants. Lunch from noon to 3 p.m., dinner from 8 p.m. to midnight.

Shops. In many places, shops are only open until lunchtime on Monday, Wednesday and Saturday. They open up for evening business, roughly 5.30 to 8 p.m., only on Tuesday, Thursday and Friday.

P

PHOTOGRAPHY (*fotografía*)

Leading brands of film and processing are available on the island but they are not cheap. It is better to bring supplies of film with you and have it processed back home. A photography shop is advertised by the sign ΦΩΤΟΓΡΑΦΕΙΟ (*fotografío*).

Hand-held photo equipment – but not tripods – may be used in museums and on archaeological sites, but you may have to pay a small fee. For security reasons, it is illegal to use a telephoto lens aboard an aircraft flying over Greece, but there are no restrictions on ordinary still, ciné- and video cameras. Photography is forbidden around Iráklion airport and in the entire Soúda Bay area.

I'd like some film for this camera.	**Tha íthela éna film giaftí ti michaní.**
black-and-white film	**asprómavro film**
colour film	**énchromo film**
35-mm film	**éna film triánda pénde milimétr**
colour slides	**énchromo film giá sláïds**
super-8	**soúper-októ**

How long will it take to develop (and print) this film?

Se póses iméres boríte na emfanísete (ke na ektypósete) aftó to film?

PLANNING YOUR BUDGET

To give you an idea of what to expect, here are some average prices in Greek drachmas (drs). However, due to inflation all prices must be regarded as *approximate*.

Babysitters. 1200-1700 drs per hour.

Bicycle hire. 500-600 drs per day, 3000-4000 drs per week.

Camping. Average prices per day: adults 400 drs, children (up to age 12) 350 drs, tents 200 drs, cars 180 drs, caravans (trailers) 300 drs.

Car hire. International company, high season July-Oct, booking on Crete): *Subaru 600*: 3500 drs per day, 50 drs per km, or 65,000 drs per week with unlimited mileage. *Opel Kadett 1.2*: 4000 drs per day, 60 drs per km, 69,000 drs per week with unlimited mileage. Add 18% tax. Advance reservations from home and smaller local companies are over 25% cheaper.

Cigarettes. Local brands 180-250 drs per packet of 20, foreign brands 250-650 drs.

Entertainment. *Bouzoúki* evening (including food) 4000 drs and up, disco from 600 drs, cinema 300-450 drs.

Hotels. (Double room with bath, summer season). Luxury: over 15,000 drs, Class A: 12,000-20,000 drs, Class B: 9000-10,000 drs, Class C: 4500-8000 drs, Class D: 2000-3500 drs.

Meals and drinks. Continental breakfast 300-400 drs, lunch or dinner in fairly good restaurants 2000 drs, coffee 150-350 drs, Greek brandy 150-250 drs, gin and tonic 400 drs, beer 150-200 drs, soft drinks 60-150 drs.

Supermarket. Bread ($^1/_2$ kg) 70 drs. Butter (250 g) 300 drs. 6 eggs 300 drs. *Féta* cheese ($^1/_2$ kg) 450 drs. Potatoes (1 kg) 80 drs. Minced meat (1 kg) 1200 drs. Soft drinks (small bottle) 70 drs.

Sports. Sailing boat 800 drs per hour. Waterskiing 4000 drs for 10 minutes. Windsurfing 900-4000 drs per hour.

Youth Hostels. Around 1000 drs per night.

POLICE (*astynomía*)

There are two kinds of police on Crete. The regular police *(chorofílakes)* are recognized by their green uniforms.

For foreign visitors in distress, there is a separate branch of the police known as *Touristikí Astynomía* (Tourist Police). On their dark-grey uniforms they wear distinctive national flag patches (Union Jack, etc) to indicate the foreign languages they speak. Tourist police have the authority to inspect prices in restaurants and hotels. If you have a complaint, these are the people to see. To get in touch with them, inquire at any tourist information office or telephone 171.

Where's the nearest police station? **Pou íne to kodinótero astynomikó tmíma?**

POST OFFICE (ΤΑΧΥΔΡΟΜΕΙΟ – *tachydromío*)

Post offices handle letters, stamps, parcels, cheque cashing, money orders and exchange, but not telephone calls (see TELEPHONE). Stamps are also on sale at news-stands and souvenir shops, but often at a 10% surcharge.

In the larger towns, the post offices have distinctive 'ΕΛ.ΤΑ' signs in yellow, the same colour as the letter boxes. In Ágios Nikólaos, the post office is located on Neapóleos Street; in Chaniá on Tzanakáki Street; in Iráklion on Platía Daskalógianni; in Réthimnon on Th. Moátsu street.

Normally, the post office clerk is obliged to check the contents of registered letters as well as parcels addressed to foreign destinations

128 so, although the formality is often waived, it is best not to seal this kind of mail until it has been 'approved'. Express special delivery service officially still exists but is nowadays too uncertain to be worth the extra charge.

A stamp for this letter/ postcard, please.	**Éna grammatósimo giaftó to grámma/kart postál, parakaló.**
airmail	**aeroporikós**
registered	**systiméno**

PUBLIC HOLIDAYS *(argíes)*

The following civil and religious holidays are observed throughout Greece with banks, offices and shops remaining closed:

Jan 1	*Protochoniá*	New Year's Day
Jan 6	*ton Theofaníon*	Epiphany
March 25	*Ikostí Pémti Martíou (tou Evangelismoú)*	Greek Independence Day
Aug 15	*Dekapendávgoustos (tis Panagías)*	Assumption Day
Oct 28	*Ikostí Ogdóï Oktovríou*	'No' *(óchi)* Day, commemorating Greek defiance of Italian invasion in 1940
Dec 25	*Christoúgenna*	Christmas Day
Dec 26	*défteri iméra ton Christougénnon*	St Stephen's Day

Movable dates of Orthodox calendar (different from Catholic and Protestant):

Katharí Deftéra	1st Day of Lent: Clean Monday
Megáli Paraskeví	Good Friday
Deftéra tou Páscha	Easter Monday
Análipsis	Ascension
tou Agíou Pnévmatos	Whit Monday (Holy Monday)

PUBLIC TRANSPORT

The island has no trains, but in general, its buses (*leoforío*) are dependable and punctual. Besides the frequent services connecting Iráklion, Ágios Nikólaos, Réthimnon and Chaniá, buses also serve all the archaeological sites and most of the island's villages. Use these vehicles – much more robust than they appear at first sight – for some of the more remote excursions and country rambles, but check times to be sure of catching the return trip. You can buy tickets in advance at the bus stations in main towns. Hold on to it as inspectors occasionally board buses to check.

bus-stop	**stásis**
When is the next bus to...?	**Póte févgi to epómeno leoforío giá...**
single (one-way)	**apló**
return (round-trip)	**me epistrofí**

R

RADIO AND TV (*rádio; tileórasi*)

Local Greek radio and TV broadcast news in English daily, but with a shortwave transistor radio you can pick up the BBC World Service and Voice of America very clearly in the evening and early morning.

Almost all hotels on the island have TV lounges (unfortunately so do many tavernas and restaurants). English-language series and films are run in the original version with Greek subtitles. Some of the bigger hotels show English-language video films.

RELIGION

The island's faith is almost 100% Greek Orthodox. There are no Anglican or other Protestant services held on Crete, nor is there a Jewish congregation. Mass is said on Saturdays, Sundays and holy days at the Catholic churches in Iráklion, Chaniá, Réthimnon and Ágios Nikólaos.

What time is mass?　　　　**Ti óra archízi i litourgía?**

TAXIS (ΤΑΞΙ – *taxí*)

Despite high fuel prices, taxis are quite cheap on Crete. The drivers are generally helpful and honest, although those in Iráklion seem gradually to be adopting the tougher, more calculating style of big city drivers everywhere.

Town taxis operate with a meter, which in the daytime should be set to '1' ('2' is the double fare for night hours, 1-5 a.m.). If there is no meter, agree on a fare before setting off. It is perfectly legitimate for a surcharge to be added at Easter and Christmas, as well as for luggage and late-night trips. Rounding up the fare is the usual way of tipping, with a little extra for special services rendered.

In the main towns, taxis are quite plentiful, both cruising and at taxi ranks, usually near the port or the bus-station. Almost every village has at least one taxi. These rural taxis are called *agoréon*.

What's the fare to...?   **Piá íne i timí giá...?**

TELEPHONES (*tiléfono*)

Each major town on Crete has an office of Greece's telecommunications organization (OTE) open daily 6 a.m. to midnight. Those in the smaller towns have shorter hours (usually 7.30 a.m. to 10 p.m., Monday to Friday). Here you can dial direct or through an operator. You can also make a local call from phone booths on the street or from news-stands. Booths sporting a large 'Telephone' sign in English usually have international dialling facilities with English-language instructions.

Greece's telephone system is reasonably modern, but the island's long-distance lines can get clogged during peak times. For important calls, let your hotel operator handle it. Fax communications are also best handled through your hotel.

Can you get me this number in...? **Boríte na mou párete aftó ton arithmó...?**

person-to-person   **prosopikí klísi**   **131**

TIME DIFFERENCES

In winter, make allowances for Greek clocks turning back one hour unless your country does the same.

What time is it?   **Ti óra íne?**

Los Angeles	Chicago	New York	London	**Crete**
2 a.m.	4 a.m.	5 a.m.	10 a.m.	**noon**

TIPPING

By law, service charges are included in the bill at hotels, restaurants and tavernas. The Greeks are not greedy, but it is the custom to leave a little extra in addition – unless, of course, the service has not been good.

Hotel-porter, per bag	50-100 drs
Maid, per day	150-200 drs
Waiter	5% (optional)
Taxi driver	10% (optional, but customary)
Tour guide ($^1/_2$ day)	150-300 drs
Lavatory attendant	30 drs

TOILETS (ΤΟΥΑΛΕΤΤΕΣ – toualéttes)

All towns of any size on the north coast have public toilets. Remember to leave a small tip if there is an attendant. In villages, try a café or taverna. If you drop in specifically to use the facilities, it is customary to have a drink before leaving. There are generally two doors: ΓΥΝΑΙΚΩΝ (ladies) and ΑΝΔΡΩΝ (men).

Where are the toilets?   **Pou íne i toualéttes?**

TOURIST INFORMATION OFFICES (grafío pliroforión tourismoú)

The following branches of the Greek National Tourist Office will supply you with brochures and maps in English. They will also show you the directory of hotels in Greece, listing all facilities and prices.

Britain: 195-197 Regent St, London W1R 8DL; tel. (071) 734 5997.

U.S.A.: 645 Fifth Ave, New York, NY 10022; tel. (212) 421 5777.
611 W. 6th St, Los Angeles, CA 90017; tel. (213) 626 6696.

In the main towns on Crete, the tourist information offices are signposted EOT *(Ellinikós Organismós Tourismoú)*.

Iráklion: across from Archaeological Museum; tel. (081) 228 203.
Réthimnon: on the seafront promenade; tel. (0831) 29148.
Chaniá: in the Mosque of the Janissaries; tel. (0821) 26426.
Ágios Nikólaos: in the port police building; tel. (0841) 22357.

Where's the tourist office?	**Pou íne to grafío tourismoú?**

W

WATER *(neró)*

Tap water is almost always safe to drink. Many find that the water served in Crete's cafés and restaurants as a chaser with ouzo or coffee is better than some of the local mineral water.

a bottle of mineral water	**éna boukáli metallikó neró**
fizzy (carbonated)/still	**me/chorís anthrakikó**
Is this drinking water?	**Íne pósimo aftó to neró?**

Y

YOUTH HOSTELS* (ΞΕΝΩΝ ΝΕΟΤΗΤΟΣ – *xenón neótitos*)

Located in or near most of the popular resorts, youth hostels offer simple but clean accommodation, though they are often not much cheaper than 'Rent Rooms' (see ACCOMMODATION). To be on the safe side, get an international membership card from your local Youth Hostel Association before leaving home, but the hostels may well let you in without one. Doors close around 10 or 11 p.m. and the maximum stay is usually five days.

Index

Numbers in bold refer to the main entry listed.

135